The Boston Basin Bicycle Book

The Boston Basin Bicycle Book

David R. Godine Boston

Nicholas Humez

Janice Goldfrank

Edward Goldfrank   Alexander Humez

First published in 1975 by
David R. Godine, Publisher
306 Dartmouth Street
Boston, Massachusetts

ISBN 0-87923-133-5
LCC 74-32579

We are grateful to the following for permission to
use their photographs: the *Boston Globe* for the
photographs on pp. 25, 39, 45, 53, 81, 117, 135,
141, and 175; Clif Garboden/the Boston *Phoenix*
for the photographs on pp. 61 and 207; Vicki
Lawrence/the Boston *Phoenix* for the photograph
on p. 201; the Museum of Transportation, Brookline, for the photograph on p. 189; Richard Merrill
for the photograph on p. 75; and Everett Tatreau
for the photograph on p. 213. The photographs on
pp. 55 and 101 are by Rachel Ritchie. All others are
by Patrick Keohane.

Printed in the United States of America

Acknowledgments

We would like to express our gratitude to the following people and institutions for their kindness in providing us with information helpful in the preparation of this book: Cathy A. of the Newton Corner News Service; the anonymous Malden fireman who acquainted us with the bicycle path in route #8; Charles Ballantyne, of the Massachusetts Department of Community Affairs; the Boston Athenaeum, the Boston Public Library (Copley Square branch), and the Boston Redevelopment Authority whose maps have been a constant and invaluable resource; Dan Cohen; the Reverend Harold T. Handley; the Historians of the Metropolitan District Commission and the town of Winchester; Clifford Kaye of the United States Geological Survey who has been most generous in giving us his time and the fruits of his research into the geological history of the Boston Basin; Arthur Krim of the Cambridge Historical Commission; Marty Landsberg; the United States Geological Survey, whose maps we have used throughout the book; and Robert Wilfong. Our gratitude, too, to Pam Riley Osborn and Phyllis Loney, who prepared the maps for publication.

We would also like to thank Betty Falsey, Alcy Frelick, Jean Humez, Jonathan Stavely, and Keith Stavely, who have cheerfully tolerated the authors' obsessive and often loud discussion of the bicycle, the Basin, and the book.

Contents

West

South

The Boston Basin Bicycle Book

The Lay of the Land:

An Introduction

This book is a collection of thirty interlocking bicycle rides. All are loops of between eight and a half and fourteen and a half miles from point of departure to point of return—START to START—and each may easily be linked with others (or pieces of others) to form any number of longer and more intricate rides. The total network of some 350 miles is designed to give a thorough sampling of the Boston Basin and the immediately surrounding highlands—roughly, the area enclosed by Route 128. (For a more precise, geological definition of the Basin, see the commentaries for routes #14 and #25 and compare the maps of bedrock geology and glacial landforms on pages 3 and 9.) All of the rides have been ridden under a variety of conditions on both three-speed and ten-speed bikes.

At the beginning of each of the five geographical sectors into which the book is divided, there appears a master route map which locates each ride in relation to both the general lay of the land and to the other rides of that region. The presentation of the individual routes of each sector gives further and more precise means of locating each ride. For openers, the title of each route tells you both where the ride lies on the map and something of its place in the long and illustrious history of the region as a whole. So, for example, the title 'Gateways to the North: Medford–Malden–Charlestown' (route #8) gives a rough idea of where the ride goes and of one of the historical roles played by the area covered by the ride in the development of the region as a whole.

After the title of each route a brief commentary follows on some feature or features characteristic of the area covered

2

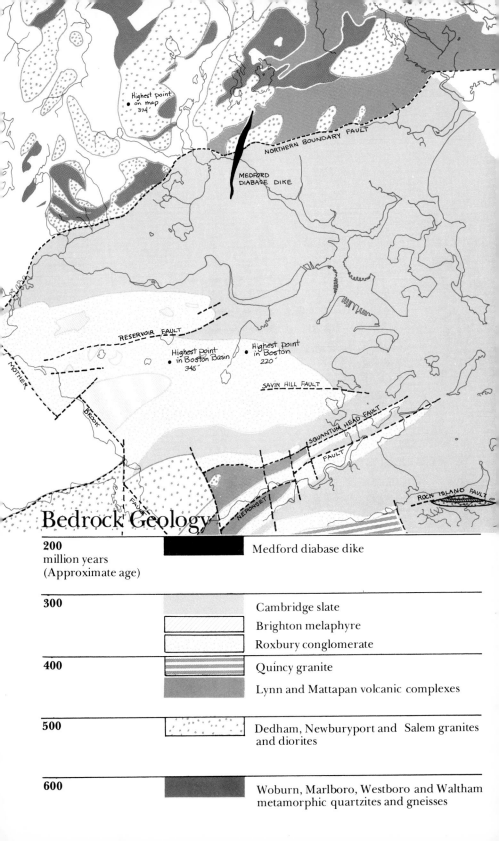

Highest point
on map
374'

NORTHERN BOUNDARY FAULT

MEDFORD
DIABASE DIKE

RESERVOIR FAULT

Highest point
in Boston Basin
345

Highest point
in Boston
220

SAVIN HILL FAULT

MOTHER

BROOK

SQUANTUM HEAD FAULT

FAULT

FAULT

ROCK ISLAND FAULT

Bedrock Geology

NEPONSET

200 million years (Approximate age)	⬛	Medford diabase dike
300		Cambridge slate
	▨	Brighton melaphyre
	▢	Roxbury conglomerate
400	▤	Quincy granite
	▨	Lynn and Mattapan volcanic complexes
500	⬚	Dedham, Newburyport and Salem granites and diorites
600	▨	Woburn, Marlboro, Westboro and Waltham metamorphic quartzites and gneisses

by the route and previewed in its title. As the network of rides has been designed to allow the rider to get a feel for the entire Boston Basin area as it is today by taking representative ten-mile samples of the terrain with its attendant sights, sounds, and smells, so the commentaries have been designed to allow the reader to get an idea of the vast web of interlocking historical processes that have combined to make the area what it is today. The samples taken in the commentaries are essentially temporal, as those taken in the actual rides are essentially spatial, though there is naturally some degree of overlap in all cases, since the rides take place in time, as history does in space. (Dramatic illustration of the complexity of this overlap is afforded by comparison of the 1776 base map on pages 6-7 with the rides in the area which it displays and with the commentaries which accompany them.) Since the span of history sampled in the commentaries stretches over some 600 million years, from the formation of the oldest rocks which can still be found in the Boston Basin to the delivery of tomorrow's newspaper in Newton, we have included an index at the end of the book to help you find your way around in time.

To help you find your way around in space, we have given two kinds of directions for each route: after each commentary there appears a set of written directions, then a map. The written route directions feature a mileage column which indicates the absolute distance from START, rounded off to the nearest tenth of a mile, at which an instruction applies. The mileages are intended to give a clear idea of the relative distances between instructions, which is a great help in avoiding missed turns in the city and, when the distance is long, in reassuring you that you *haven't* missed a turn, as you were perhaps beginning to fear.

Rather than list the mileages next to the instructions which follow closely on each others' heels, we use a set of verbal conventions which give a rough, impressionistic indication of the different distances between successive instructions. By using such phrases as

mi. 2.1   BEAR RIGHT onto TALBOT ST., then immediately LEFT onto WASHINGTON ST.

and

we try to show how quickly things are about to happen. Further information is also helpful at times, owing to any number of oddities in the Greater Boston street system: street signs periodically disappear or get spun around by careless drivers and malicious passers-by; streets change names at intersections and town lines, not always obviously or consistently. Here we do the best we can: 'RIGHT onto MARSHALL ST. (over railroad bridge) (becomes PARK ST., Saugus).'

The maps which accompany the routes serve two purposes. First, of course, they show where the rides go. They also tell you something interesting or useful about the region in which the ride lies, and as such are quite on a par with the route commentaries. As the commentaries tell you what happened in the route's region, the maps show you where it all happened and, often, why. You could probably form as full a picture of the area's history by browsing through these maps as you could by performing a similar operation on the commentaries or on the inventory of rides themselves.

This brings us to the question of sampling the samples. The rides, commentaries, and maps are all samples of one sort or another: the rides go down some streets but not others, the commentaries are snapshots of history rather than a multi-dimensional moving picture, and a map that tried to show you *everything* would be utterly unreadable in its complexity. Samples can be enjoyed in two ways: for themselves, and as constituents of a larger and more intricate entity. In any case, you can count on getting more out of each route you ride each time you ride it.

As 'The Fifty Reasons Route' (route #2) makes abundantly clear, it is possible to write, for any ride of about ten miles, a points-of-interest list about a mile long. The more you develop your familiarity with a particular route, or route subset, the more you are bound to notice all of the things to come back to look at more closely when time and your frame of mind allow, or, as in a case like that offered by route #15 ('Lexington: This Way to the Parade Route'),

Roads and Wetlands of 1776

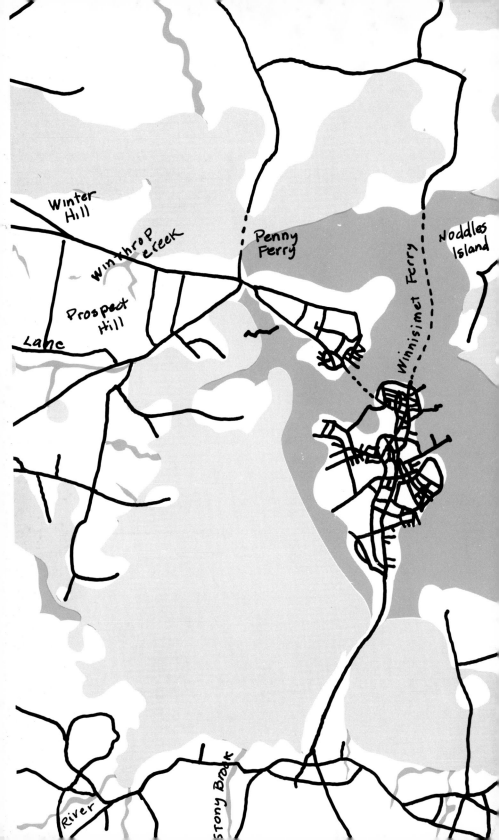

when a special event is scheduled. Thus, an out-of-the-way museum or old house which charges admission might bring you back again with money, while such potential time-consumers as Harvard's Peabody Museum, which is free to all who travel route #3 and which has a spectacular diorama of the Boston Basin *circa* 1900, may be enjoyed again and again at leisure.

Increased familiarity with a route not only tells you where to stop and investigate, but when to go for the fullest (and safest) sampling. 'When to go' can be seasonal or multi-seasonal: the rides on the rim of the wheel whose hub is Boston should be ridden in the fall for the foliage, if at no other time and for no other reason; and virtually all of the rides are best appreciated when ridden for comparison in different seasons. If you spot some wild iris in a roadside ditch on route #14 in late May, by all means go back in July for the dazzling purple loosestrife; and the raw solitude of the beaches of Revere, East Boston, South Boston, and Quincy before and after the swimming season should be compared with their summer crowds and bustle for a realistic picture of these regions.

'When to go' can, of course, be more precisely specified, for some times of the week and some times of the day are better than others. The urban routes of the central sector (the Hub) are at their least hair-raising early Sunday morning, when most of the local traffic is going to or from church and the daily commuters are at home in the suburbs. (Towns in which a substantial segment of the population keeps the Sabbath on Saturday can be ridden in similarly relaxed fashion on that day — see routes #20, #21, and #26.) Route #2 is especially recommended as a Sunday ride, as it is on this day the residents of both the North End and Chinatown take to the streets to socialize. (In Boston, as in most American cities, Sunday is also the big marketing day in Chinatown.) Rides like route #18 can be ridden without the distraction of heavy traffic at virtually any time of the day on any day except during rush hour, which here, as elsewhere, comes twice every weekday from about 7:30 to 9:00 A.M. and 3:30 to 6:00 P.M. (with slight peaks at 2:30 and 3:00 when school lets out). When *not* to go, then, is during the afternoon rush hour on Monday when motor vehicle

operators on their way home tend to be at their least attentive and their most hostile.

Further familiarity with a route and with the area through which it passes allows the enterprising cyclist to work out any number of route variants for even fuller sampling. The area covered by a route may be expanded by the simple addition of another route, a piece of a route, or a loop composed of streets not on any of the routes. (The figure-eight that can be made by joining routes #17 and #18 is especially recommended, as are the various combinations of routes #1, #3, and #4 that sample the city of Cambridge.) The area covered by a route can be made smaller and more select by patching together route pieces or by the judicious use of cross-streets, or both. (The most promising area for route-piecing is the central sector, in which route #7 intersects no fewer than eleven routes at seventeen different points, while the most leisurely experiments in cross-street route abbreviation may be undertaken on route #20.) Finally, the area covered by a route may be held constant while the direction from which it is approached may be changed. Some routes, generally the more suburban ones like #15 and #18, may be ridden in their entirety in the reverse direction from that given in this book. Most, however, cannot or should not be ridden in the reverse direction without modification, given such thoroughly human inventions as the one-way street and the treacherous left-hand turn across traffic.

It is hoped that this book will be seen not simply as a catalogue of thirty bicycle rides in and around the relatively small area of the Boston Basin, but as the exemplary presentation of a strategy — or set of strategies — for the safe and enjoyable investigation of *any* 'here' and 'there' connected by at least one two-way street. There are, after all, well over 9 million square miles, much of it paved and much of that open to cyclists, to be pedaled on the continent of North America alone after you've finished with the area within Route 128. Larger and more numerous samples are *always* possible.

1   The Duck (To Water)

Along the Charles

We put this ride first because it's a good introduction to both the Boston Basin and this book. It takes you over the three kinds of terrain that have made the area what it is today: water, land, and land fill. It gives an idea of the range of traffic conditions and types of scenery the region offers. And it provides a sampling of our particular interests: visible history, pleasant scenery, and easy cycling.

The ride begins on original terra firma just outside Harvard Square, formerly the center of 'Newe Towne,' Lieutenant Governor Dudley's candidate for the capital of the Massachusetts Bay Colony. In theory, 'Newe Towne' made an ideal capital since it was both easy to protect and close to the harbor. In practice, it had three strikes against it from the outset. First, it was a compromise location, chosen after other officials of the new colony had settled elsewhere. Second, 'protection' turned out to be unnecessary and only created an issue when the other settlements were taxed to fortify 'Newe Towne.' Third, it was a long and inconvenient haul to Boston, which was where the governor, John Winthrop, lived. It was eventually arranged for the government, and not the governor, to move, making Boston the official capital.

But all was not lost for 'Newe Towne,' for in 1637, as a consolation prize, it was decreed that 'a schoale or colledge' should be built there 'to advance learning and to perpetuate it to posterity. . . . ' The town was promptly renamed 'Cambridge' after everybody's alma mater back home. Shortly thereafter, John Harvard died, leaving £800 and his personal library to the 'colledge,' thereby securing his place in history.

From the Larz Anderson Bridge (an updated version of the oldest bridge across the Charles River) to where you pick up Brookline St. (some seven miles later), you are almost exclusively on non-original land, as a glance at the route map readily shows. Made land has a number of interesting characteristics. First, of course, it tends to be flat: it's a nuisance to have to lug all of that fill from wherever you got it to wherever the new land is being made, and the more you use, the farther afield you will eventually have to go for it. Operations in Cambridge and Boston quickly leveled the few unsettled nearby drumlins, so a lot of the land in the area today came by train from Needham.

Another characteristic of made land is this: because it's so costly, it tends to be undertaken by not just anybody and, consequently, tends to have not just anything built on it. The Cambridge land fill on this route has some heavy industry and MIT, a land-grant college, believe it or not. On both the Cambridge and Boston fill rest the major roads (and, more recently, the major bike paths) which follow the Charles. If you look closely at the far (Boston) side of Storrow Drive, you will see the retaining wall which lines much of the Charles. Behind this wall is Beacon St. and the Back Bay, which was filled in the 1800's by the water power companies that had dammed the Back Bay years earlier, the Commonwealth of Massachusetts, and the City of Boston, to house all of those people who might otherwise have moved to Cambridge and other surrounding towns, lowering the Boston tax-base.

When you arrive at Brookline St., you are again on original land. The next street over on the left is Magazine St., so called because there used to be a powder magazine at the river end of the street during the Revolution. Handy to the magazine is Fort Washington. (Fort Washington makes more sense if you remember that everything between it and the Charles rests on post-Revolutionary land fill.) What were the British doing, one wonders, that the revolutionaries could feel free to set up shop just across the river? (Washington's headquarters were no farther away than just outside Harvard Square.) If it's a long and inconvenient haul from Cambridge to Boston, how much more so if you were going in the opposite direction and people were shooting at you?

1 Directions

START	Intersection of BOYLSTON ST. and MEMORIAL DR., Cambridge.
mi. 0.0	EAST on MDC BIKE PATH (between river and Memorial Dr.)
2.4	CROSS MASSACHUSETTS AVE. (path stops, then starts again)
3.0	JOIN CAMBRIDGE PKWY. (just before Longfellow Bridge) STRAIGHT on CAMBRIDGE PKWY. (under bridge)
3.9	RIGHT onto CAMBRIDGE ST.
4.2	RIGHT onto MDC BIKE PATH (at end of bridge)
6.7	CROSS BU FOOTBRIDGE (over Storrow Dr., carrying bike), then RIGHT onto PARKING LOT DRIVEWAY (river to right)
6.9	LEFT onto UNIVERSITY RD., then RIGHT onto COMMONWEALTH AVE.
7.0	RIGHT onto BU BRIDGE
7.2	STRAIGHT across bridge onto BROOKLINE ST. (under overpass)
7.5	RIGHT onto ERIE ST.
7.7	RIGHT onto WAVERLY ST. LEFT, RIGHT, then LEFT 3/4 around FORT WASHINGTON PARK, then LEFT back onto WAVERLY ST.
8.0	RIGHT onto PUTNAM AVE.
9.1	LEFT onto MASSACHUSETTS AVE.
9.5	BEAR LEFT (at HARVARD SQ. KIOSK) onto BRATTLE ST., then STRAIGHT across BOYLSTON ST. on BRATTLE ST.
9.6	BEAR LEFT onto ELLIOT ST. (Brattle forks right), then CROSS MT. AUBURN ST. on ELLIOT ST.
9.8	RIGHT onto BOYLSTON ST. to
9.9	START.

Peddling pretzels in Harvard Square

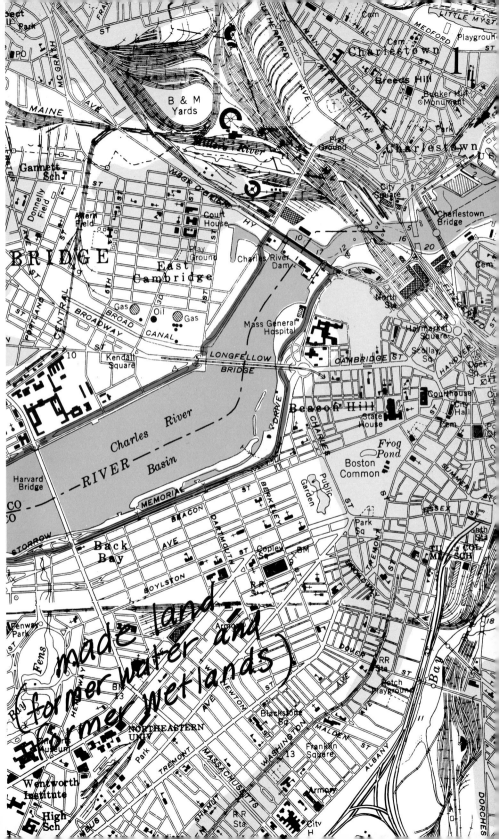

2　Old Boston

The Fifty Reasons Route

An axiom: it is always a good idea to have at least two compelling reasons for going somewhere so that, should one of them prove to be a dud, you will at least have the other to fall back on and the trip will not have been a total loss. And if all goes well, you will have gotten the enjoyment of two trips for the price of one. There are at least fifty compelling reasons to ride this route. In order of appearance, they are:

1　Harvard Bridge (intersection of Mass. Ave. and Memorial Drive) and immediate vicinity (in which there are shaded benches). Best views of Boston across the Charles River, and an excellent people-viewing location. MIT students periodically mark off the bridge in Smoots, the original Smoot (now preserved in the Smithsonian Institution) having been an MIT fraternity pledge who was end-over-ended from one end of the bridge to the other.

2　MIT (along Memorial Drive).

3　Longfellow Bridge (with the salt and pepper shakers and subway). Second-best views of Boston across the Charles.

4, 5　Old Lechmere Canal and New Prison Point Bridge. (The latter involves a slight but highly rewarding detour over the bridge and back at Cambridge St. Use the sidewalk on the left, as it's safer and has all the reading material.)

6　The Boston Museum of Science (Cambridge St.), from which you also get a good view of the Bunker Hill Monument.

7　Causeway St., which has on it North Station, a section of the El (elevated railway), a turnpike entrance, and the Charlestown Bridge, all in the space of a (large) block. At the bridge and after, there are good views of Charlestown and the harbor. Causeway St. runs across what was once a natural harbor between Beacon Hill and Copps Hill. The street was originally an Indian path across mud flats. It was subsequently made first into a mill dam, then filled in (except for a canal at Canal St.), then really filled in.

8   Old Boston Waterfront (part the first). The old Boston waterfront ran between Copps Hill and Fort Hill. Note that the warehouses are parallel to the waterfront rather than perpendicular to it (as farther down the street). Parallel implies a lower volume of activity than perpendicular, since parallel parking allows fewer ships to dock than does perpendicular.

9   The North End. This neighborhood has housed a large Italian-speaking population for over a hundred years. (One of the benefits of cycling is that you get to *hear* the place you're visiting.)

10   Brick park with equestrian statue of Paul Revere (Hanover St.).

11   The New North Church (St. Stephen's) (across the street from the park).

12   Italian bakeries.

13   Old North Church (Christ Church) of one-if-by-land, two-if-by-sea fame (Salem St.).

14   Copps Hill Burying Ground (a short detour up Hull St. on foot because it's one way going the wrong way).

15   Good views of Charlestown, Chelsea, and East Boston (Charter St.).

16   Another strange (stone) park (Charter St.).

17   Old wharves and the Old Boston Waterfront (part the second) (Commercial St.–Atlantic Ave.). Note urban renewal which here, as elsewhere, means converting old buildings into expensive housing. Note also that the old stone warehouses are more nearly fireproof than their wooden cousins and that they are perpendicular to the waterfront.

18   Good view of the Custom House. (Ships coming into the harbor used to aim for it.)

19   Long Wharf (formerly King's Wharf). This was the

main wharf in the harbor and today affords great views of the harbor islands, East Boston, Chelsea, South Boston, and the water.

20   Harbor cruises and boat trips to Provincetown (leaving from Long Wharf).

21   The Boston Aquarium (Atlantic Ave.).

22   The Boston Tea Party Ship and Museum (Congress St.).

23   The bridge to South Boston (Congress St.).

24   South Station (Summer St.). Not much to look at, but it forms a boxed set with North Station and you might as well enjoy it while it lasts.

25   Old retail section (Summer St.–Chauncy St.).

26   Chinatown (complete with bilingual street signs). As the North End forms a population center at the base of Copps Hill, so do Chinatown and the South End form a population center at the base of Fort Hill (which no longer exists as such, having been removed for use as land fill).

27   Washington Street and the 'Combat Zone,' the home of the penny arcades, the X-rated movies, and one of the strangest collections of people in the city.

28   Park Square. This intersection is the peculiar shape it is because it marks the inevitable coming together of the streets laid out by the Commonwealth of Massachusetts and those laid out by the City of Boston in their nominally cooperative filling in of the Back Bay. The Commonwealth built its part parallel with present-day Beacon St. while the City built *its* part parallel with Washington St. Beacon St. and Washington St. run at a 45-degree tilt to each other.

29   The Public Garden (Charles St.).

30   The swan boats (in the Public Garden).

31   Boston Common (Charles St.).

32   Charles St. (which used to front on the Charles River — thus, everything to your left was once under water). Charles St. runs along the base of the fanciest side of Beacon Hill, the last of the three original English population centers in Boston.

33   Louisburg Square (off Mt. Vernon St.). The last original land to be developed for housing in Boston.

34   The Church of the Advent (Brimmer St.).

35   Longfellow Bridge (again), Charles St. subway station, and the Charles St. Jail.

36   Views of the not-so-fancy side of Beacon Hill. When Louisburg Square was built (expressly for the wealthy), the not-so-fancy side of the hill was already there as housing for the city's labor force (or that part of it not living on the other two hills). The streets on the hill were laid out in such a way that even today it takes a great deal of imagination and determination to get from one side to the other.

37   Museum of the Gray Otis House (Cambridge St.).

38   Old West Church (Cambridge St.).

39, 40   Bowdoin Square and Scollay Square (Cambridge St.). Boston has a number of squares whose raison d'être seems to be their proximity to other squares rather than any special attraction of the square itself. These are usually 'Y squares,' one prong of which goes to another 'Y square.' Such 'assistant' squares as these turn out, not surprisingly, to make great mass transit connectors. Scollay Sq. was once *the* terminus for the stagecoach lines, and Bowdoin Sq. was the place to catch the trolley to Cambridge if you were coming from East Boston, Chelsea, or Scollay Sq. Scollay Sq. has since been metamorphosed to Government Center.

41   New City Hall and Government Center Plaza. Interesting architecture, several good places to eat and drink, and excellent for people-watching. The top floor of New City Hall affords good views and houses the Boston Redevelopment Authority, where a variety of maps of the area may be obtained.

42   King's Chapel Graveyard and King's Chapel, whose names give an accurate idea of their antiquity (Tremont St.).

43   Old Granary Burying Ground (Tremont St.).

44   Park St. subway station and Boston Common (intersection of Park St. and Tremont St.), the heart of the Boston subway system and a gathering ground for all sorts of interesting people.

45   The State House (intersection of Park St. and Beacon St.).

2

46 The Boston Athenaeum (a few doors down to the right on Beacon St.).

47 The Archives Museum (Beacon St., next door to the State House).

48 The site of John Hancock's house (Beacon St.).

49 Beacon St. (from Charles St. to Mass. Ave.). Originally part of the Charles River, later a mill dam and causeway, to which the Commonwealth made parallel streets as it did its share of the filling in of the Back Bay. Look left to see what became of the Bay; right, for glimpses of Cambridge across the Charles River.

50 Harvard Bridge, for the other view.

Copyright © 1975, Norman Hurst

Salvatore Sambuco, the 'Crab Man' of the North End

2 Directions

5.6   STRAIGHT onto ELIOT ST. (Stuart St. forks left)
5.7   RIGHT onto BROADWAY (at Park Sq.)
5.8   BEAR LEFT onto CHARLES ST.
6.2   RIGHT onto MT. VERNON ST.
6.4   RIGHT onto WALNUT ST., then RIGHT onto CHESTNUT ST.
6.6   RIGHT onto CHARLES ST.
6.8   LEFT onto PINCKNEY ST., then LEFT onto BRIMMER ST.

Copyright © 1975, Norman Hurst

6.9   LEFT onto MT. VERNON ST.
7.0   LEFT onto CHARLES ST.
7.2   BEAR RIGHT onto CAMBRIDGE ST. (becomes TREMONT ST.)
8.0   RIGHT onto PARK ST.
8.2   LEFT onto BEACON ST.
9.6   RIGHT onto MASSACHUSETTS AVE. to
10.0 START.

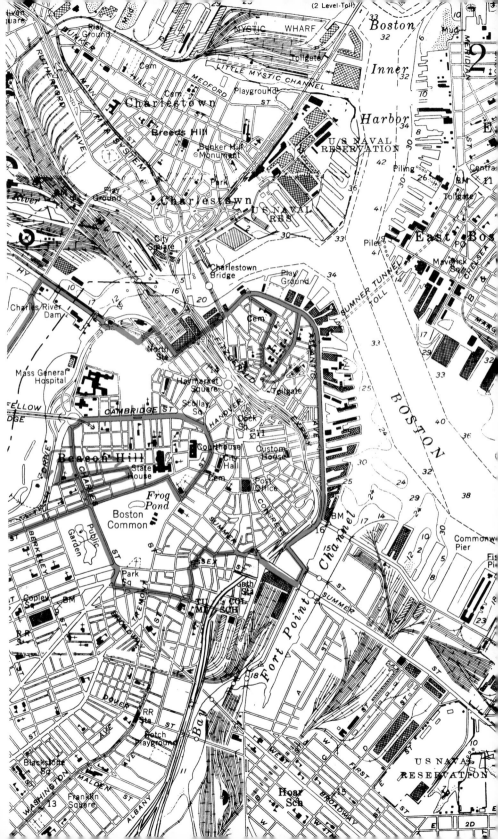

3   The Red Brick Sidewalks

Cambridge

At the turn of this century, the City of Cambridge embarked on an ambitious 'practical beautification' program, which involved laying granite curbstone and red brick sidewalk and planting elm trees along all of its then-existing streets. Curbstone helps keep the street and the sidewalk in their respective places, and granite is hard (and plentiful). Elms are good city trees because they have relatively long trunks and provide lots of shade. And red brick? Well, the last continental ice sheet was so heavy that the crust of the earth sank under its weight (over one thousand feet under the thickest part in Canada and northern Europe, but only fifty feet near its southern edge around Boston). When the ice melted and returned its water to the sea, the depressed land was flooded before it had a chance to recover. Marine clay (red only after baking, gray-brown before) was left all over Cambridge, the last glacially caused imprint on the land. The brick companies, once booming in Cambridge, got the final word by stamping their hallmarks into some of their bricks.

The red brick sidewalk network as it exists today provides an interesting reflection of the city, both past and present. Here are some things that have happened to red brick sidewalks in Cambridge and what this tells you about the city. First, of course, nothing much happens to red brick sidewalks if large numbers of people don't walk on them and the trees planted beside them have someplace to send their roots besides up. Sidewalks that don't see much foot traffic tend to be found (a) in quiet residential neighborhoods and (b) near warehouses and factory outlets, where trucks hold a virtual monopoly on the traffic.

Red brick sidewalks which *do* see a fair amount of foot traffic tend to wear out eventually, especially when helped along by claustrophobic tree roots. Such sidewalks also tend to get 'fixed' in fairly short order. 'Fixed' here nearly always means 'paved,' partly because there's less clay in the area than there once was, partly because paving technology has improved, and partly because slightly worn brick, especially when covered with wet leaves, is not the easiest hiking terrain in the world, whatever its aesthetic merits. (There are a few new red brick sidewalks, though, and these form an interesting subset.) The oldest local sidewalk paving is concrete, and then came asphalt.

You are now ready to be your own urban archaeologist, able to make all kinds of inferences about the volume of foot traffic — and all that that implies — in and around Cambridge at various periods of history. For you can make some very good guesses about how it was and how it is simply by seeing what the sidewalk is made of and, where more than the top layer is visible, what underlies it. Two final reminders for the urban archaeologist: new streets have been built (with sidewalks) since the original red brick project was completed, and, on old streets, great chunks of sidewalk have been removed to allow modern piping to be put in from the street, the moral being that you should always take an 'adequate' sample before making your inferences. A few blocks should do.

3 Directions

START	Intersection of BU BRIDGE and MEMORIAL DR., Cambridge.
mi. 0.0	NORTH onto BROOKLINE ST. (under overpass)
0.2	LEFT onto CHESTNUT ST.
0.4	RIGHT onto MAGAZINE ST.
0.9	LEFT onto GREEN ST., then immediately RIGHT onto RIVER ST.
1.0	CROSS MASSACHUSETTS AVE. onto PROSPECT ST.
1.2	LEFT onto HARVARD ST.
2.0	RIGHT onto PRESCOTT ST.
2.1	LEFT onto BROADWAY, then RIGHT onto QUINCY ST.
2.2	LEFT onto KIRKLAND ST.
2.3	RIGHT onto OXFORD ST.
3.0	LEFT onto PRENTISS ST.
3.1	RIGHT onto MASSACHUSETTS AVE.
3.3	LEFT onto UPLAND RD.
3.7	BEAR LEFT on UPLAND RD.
3.8	RIGHT onto HURON AVE.
4.1	BEAR RIGHT on HURON AVE. (at Wyman Sq.)
4.7	CROSS FRESH POND PARKWAY to sidewalk, then RIGHT along sidewalk
4.8	LEFT into FRESH POND PARK, then LEFT around 1 circuit of pond on BIKE PATH
7.1	EXIT from Park and RETURN to HURON AVE. via sidewalk
7.2	LEFT onto HURON AVE.
7.6	RIGHT onto LAKE VIEW AVE.
7.9	LEFT onto BRATTLE ST.
8.8	LEFT onto MASON ST.
8.9	RIGHT onto GARDEN ST.
9.1	RIGHT onto MASSACHUSETTS AVE., then
9.2	RIGHT onto BRATTLE ST. (at kiosk), then first
9.3	LEFT onto MT. AUBURN ST.

9.7   STRAIGHT onto MASSACHUSETTS AVE.
       (at Putnam Ave.)

3

10.3   RIGHT onto BAY ST.
10.4   LEFT onto FRANKLIN ST.
10.8   RIGHT onto PEARL ST.
11.5   LEFT onto GRANITE ST.
11.6   RIGHT onto BROOKLINE ST. and
       CROSS MEMORIAL DRIVE (under overpass)
       to
11.7   START.

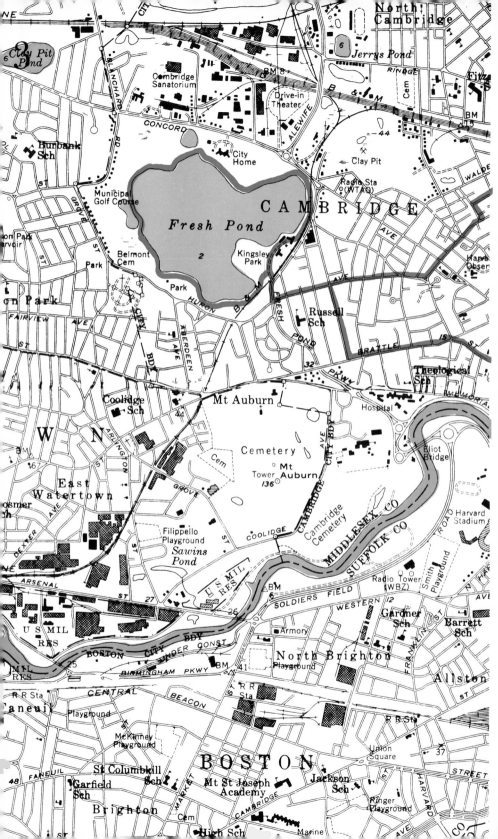

4 Flatland

Industrial Cambridge–Charlestown–Somerville

To some people, flat terrain is the best kind. It's easier, for example, to lay railroad track, build roads, and land airplanes where it's flat than where it's not; and it's easier to construct the buildings to house the industries serviced by the railroads, trucking companies, and airplanes so conveniently placed nearby. This love of the plane is not, of course, universal. It is no fun to live really close to industrial flatland because of the noise and trembling caused by the heavy traffic in the air and on the land. And if, as in the area of Cambridge surrounding MIT, white-collar industry moves in, displacing many of the former employers of blue-collar workers, it's not so great to live on the periphery of flatland either; rents go up and jobs disappear.

Land is made flat in two ways: the parts that stick up are removed, and the holes are filled in. Both of these are natural processes which humans have learned how to help along, sometimes in one step: drumlins make excellent land fill. What nature will eventually accomplish if left to its own devices can be hastened with shovels and carts or their descendants, the steam-shovel and the dump-truck. And, of course, a ready supply of money, as land-filling projects are usually large and expensive.

Much of the area covered in this ride is on made land, formerly tidal wetlands of the Charles River, which began to be filled in and built upon in the latter half of the nineteenth century. (Many of the buildings have their construction dates, mostly ca. 1900, prominently displayed on their façades.) Prison Point Bridge spans what was once Miller's River, later the start of the Middlesex Canal, and now the railroad yards for the Boston & Maine.

In Charlestown and Somerville, you're back on original land, as might be guessed from the hills and the houses built upon them. Medford St. (Somerville)–Gore St. (Cambridge) recrosses the memory of Miller's River into East Cambridge, formerly Lechmere's Point. Windsor St. crosses over the top of what was once Pelham's Island. At Sidney St., you are once again on original land at the damp edge of Old Cambridgeport.

A final attribute of urban flatland of especial interest to the cyclist should be mentioned here. Because of the heavy truck traffic — the trucks are heavy and, during certain hours, the traffic is too — the road surface is in virtually constant need of repair, so watch out for potholes. These turn out to be quite interesting to look at, as they afford an excellent view of the history of road-paving technology: several strata may frequently lie exposed at once, since large vehicles make large holes. The size of the potholes is only in keeping with the generally large scale of things in urban flatland: large buildings with large signs on them, large empty lots where large buildings used to stand before they were torn down to make room for new ones, and long views down long, straight streets. And there are very few smalls around, besides the cyclist, to provide a 'normal' yardstick.

4

4 Directions

START	Intersection of BU BRIDGE and MEMORIAL DR., Cambridge.
mi. 0.0	NORTH on BROOKLINE ST.
0.2	RIGHT onto HENRY ST.
0.4	LEFT onto WAVERLY ST.
0.5	RIGHT onto ERIE ST.
0.6	LEFT onto ALBANY ST.
1.0	CROSS MASSACHUSETTS AVE. on ALBANY ST.
1.4	RIGHT onto MAIN ST.
1.5	LEFT onto SIXTH ST.
1.6	RIGHT onto BROADWAY
1.8	RIGHT onto MAIN ST.
1.9	RIGHT onto PELHAM ST.
2.0	LEFT onto BROADWAY
2.2	RIGHT onto FULKERSON ST.
2.3	RIGHT onto BINNEY ST.
2.9	LEFT onto FIRST ST.
3.3	RIGHT onto CAMBRIDGE ST.
3.5	WALK bike LEFT over PRISON POINT BRIDGE (at Commercial St.)
4.0	STRAIGHT onto AUSTIN ST.
4.2	LEFT onto MAIN ST.
5.0	BEAR LEFT, then RIGHT (past Schrafft's) on MAIN ST., then LEFT (toward the roundhouse), then
5.2	BEAR LEFT onto CAMBRIDGE ST. (signs for Cambridge) (becomes WASHINGTON ST., Somerville)
6.3	RIGHT onto COLUMBUS AVE.
6.5	RIGHT onto PROSPECT HILL PARKWAY to the Citadel, then BACK to COLUMBUS AVE., going
6.6	STRAIGHT onto STONE AVE.
6.8	LEFT onto SOMERVILLE AVE.
6.9	RIGHT onto MEDFORD ST.
7.1	LEFT onto GORE ST. (becomes SOUTH ST., Cambridge)
7.3	RIGHT onto SIXTH ST.
7.4	LEFT onto OTIS ST.

7.7	RIGHT onto SECOND ST.
8.0	RIGHT onto CHARLES ST.
8.3	LEFT onto SIXTH ST.
8.4	RIGHT onto BINNEY ST.
8.7	RIGHT onto PORTLAND ST.
8.8	LEFT onto PLYMOUTH ST.
9.0	LEFT onto WINDSOR ST.
9.5	RIGHT onto MASSACHUSETTS AVE., then LEFT onto LANSDOWNE ST.
9.6	RIGHT onto GREEN ST.
9.8	LEFT onto SIDNEY ST.
10.4	RIGHT onto HENRY ST.
10.5	LEFT onto BROOKLINE ST. to
10.7	START.

The potholes of Broadway, Cambridge

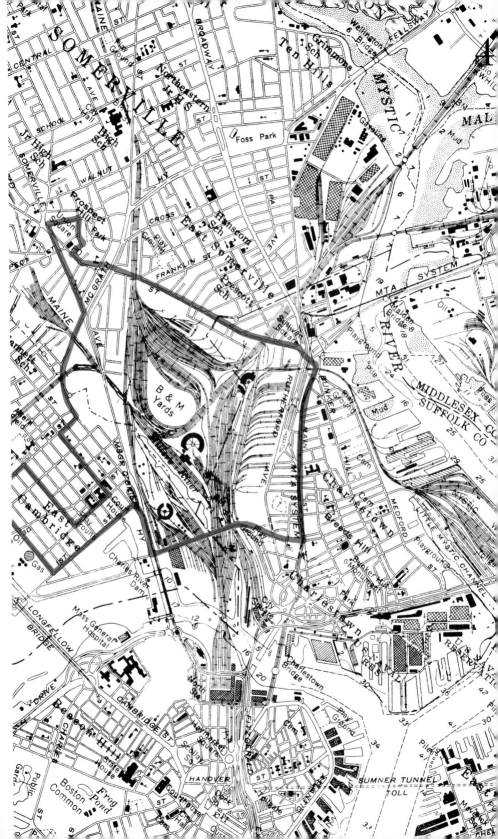

5   The Emerald Necklace

Charles River to Jamaica Pond

Since the post–Civil War era when Frederick Law Olmsted promoted the plans for a continuous green belt from Boston Common to Franklin Park, many of the jewels have been plucked from his 'Emerald Necklace' to be recut and placed in less expensive settings. Nevertheless, considering the obstacles which Olmsted overcame to get all the jewels onto one string in the first place, his linear park has aged quite well. Riding along its sinuous paths or stopping to take advantage of the public privacy offered by its benches is a good time to reflect on just what parks are and how they come into being.

First of all, parks are the product of planning and promotion. For all its apparent 'naturalness,' the Back Bay Fens are just as manmade as the rest of the Back Bay. As the suburbanization of America got up steam after the Civil War, land-filling and street-paving messed up natural drainage so much that the Muddy River had become an open sewer with the unfortunate tendency to overflow its banks. The anticipated rise in the value of the land around this nuisance was one of the selling points of the plan to transform the Fens into a flood control basin disguised as a park.

Second, parks are land, and land use is one of the things that politics is all about, since the concept of property (private and public) is central to our legal system. The benefits of stringing Franklin Park into the necklace were much less obvious to the patronage-ridden Boston city government than they were to Olmsted. The way in which pushing boulders and trees around on this high ground would work to raise tax assessments of adjoining property was not as tangible as putting in a few streets and building tax-paying houses. Even the argument that both the land and the labor to transform it into a rural park could be had at bargain rates during the postwar depression did not speed the government into large spending to stimulate the economy. In the end, however, Olmsted made his point with the backing of Boston's wealthy, philanthropic establishment.

A park represents the working out of many conflicts. In one way or another, these boil down to the time-tested opposition of long-run versus short-run. Olmsted's early career was one of political activism, first as a theoretician in the antislavery movement, then as a landscape architect trying to get short-run opportunistic city governments to be responsive to the humanitarian concerns requiring long-run planning. His parks are design statements of his beliefs about how a society should be organized and run.

America's population expanded rapidly throughout the nineteenth century and metropolises grew faster than their governments could readjust the scope of their authority. The opportunities for small-scale real estate speculation on the fringes of advancing cities defined the political checker game played out on the emerging street pattern. The game was generally as irregular as the board. Olmsted's meandering roads and rural vistas are explicit opposites of the rectilinear grid loved by developers and encouraged by city policy.

Romantic park designs expressed Olmsted's sense of loss of political harmony in ethnicized, industrialized America. The phrasing of his message and the scale of his work were very much in keeping with the times. Many of the land-use principles which he developed (such as the need for continual, long-range planning) are still applicable today, though the number of checkers has increased so drastically that there's not enough room for them all on the old board.

Planners attempting to provide for adequate open space today are looking at ways in which the typical urban grid street pattern causes inefficient land use. By experimenting with grids of different sizes and shapes, new building

5

patterns can be developed which release large areas for other uses, such as for parks, without changing the basic floor space available. But planners are rarely called in until it's too late for planning, and people with Olmsted's political clout rarely go into the park business these days, so until such time as cyclists rule the world, we must appreciate open spaces where we find them and carry our parks along with us the rest of the time.

A perambulation in the Back Bay Fens

5 Directions

START	Boston side of HARVARD BRIDGE (MASSACHUSETTS AVE.).
mi. 0.0	SOUTHEAST on MASSACHUSETTS AVE.
0.3	RIGHT onto BOYLSTON ST.
0.5	BEAR RIGHT onto FENWAY, then LEFT onto ROUTE 1 South, then
0.6	LEFT onto BIKE PATH
0.8	MERGE RIGHT with SIDEWALK
0.9	JOIN ROUTE 1 South (PARK DR.)
1.5	CROSS BROOKLINE AVE. in middle lane, then PASS SEARS ROEBUCK AND CO., then LEFT onto MDC BIKE PATH
2.3	BEAR LEFT onto NETHERLANDS RD., then BEAR LEFT onto PARKWAY RD.
2.4	RIGHT onto BROOKLINE AVE., then (at light) LEFT across BROOKLINE AVE., then RIGHT onto BIKE PATH
2.5	LEFT, then RIGHT onto ROUTE 1 South
2.7	RIGHT (first exit), then HAIRPIN LEFT onto BIKE PATH
3.0	BEAR LEFT, then STRAIGHT on MIDDLE PATH (at end of pavement)
3.2	LEFT onto pavement
3.3	RIGHT onto ROUTE 1 South
3.5	SLIGHT RIGHT into Park on BIKE PATH
4.6	LEFT onto PERKINS ST. (at intersection of Parkman Dr. and Perkins St.) (becomes COTTAGE ST.)
4.8	BEAR LEFT onto GODDARD AVE.
5.8	HAIRPIN LEFT onto NEWTON ST.
6.0	LEFT into LARZ ANDERSON PARK (follow one-way signs)
6.4	LEFT onto AVON ST.
6.6	RIGHT onto GODDARD AVE. BEAR RIGHT onto COTTAGE ST.
7.6	LEFT onto CHESTNUT ST., then

RIGHT onto RIVERDALE PARKWAY DR.

8.4 WALK BIKE across WASHINGTON ST. to RIVER RD. (directly opposite) STRAIGHT on RIVER RD

8.5 BEAR LEFT onto BROOKLINE AVE.

8.9 LEFT onto RIVERWAY (= Route 1 North)

9.6 STRAIGHT across BROOKLINE AVE. onto FENWAY

10.1 BEAR LEFT on FENWAY

10.6 BEAR RIGHT through GATE, then LEFT onto HEMENWAY ST.

10.8 RIGHT onto BOYLSTON ST.

11.0 LEFT onto HEREFORD ST.

11.2 LEFT onto COMMONWEALTH AVE. (keep right)

11.3 RIGHT onto MASSACHUSETTS AVE. to

11.5 START.

F. L. Olmsted's Original Plan for the Emerald Necklace Park System

6 The New Land

Back Bay to Pleasure Bay and Back

The Back Bay is already so famous for its extravagance that an attempt to describe it here would be useless: the loop along Massachusetts Ave., Berkeley St., and Commonwealth Ave. should provide a representative sample of the visible aspects of the neighborhood.

When industrial growth, population increase, and immigration burst the seams of Boston in the mid-1800's, the city government attempted to maintain its tax-base and keep the prosperous close at hand by managing development on the periphery of the city. Several projects in the new South End on both sides of narrow Boston Neck were undertaken or authorized by the city to fill in and improve public lands. The Commonwealth had already authorized the construction of a mill dam across the Back Bay in the hopes of providing tidal power for factories but, when the power project failed, they too became interested in filling and developing land.

A political fight between the Commonwealth and the City of Boston arose immediately and the two factions devoted considerable energy to real estate competition. Back Bay streets were laid out by the Commonwealth parallel to the mill dam (present-day Beacon St.), while South End streets were lined up with Washington St. by the City. The conflict between the City and the Commonwealth, combined with disparate sewage and flooding problems as a result of the filling, and the natural division created by the Providence and Worcester Railroad, led to different kinds of neighborhood developing on either side.

Back Bay was close to Beacon Hill, but the new South End

was merely an extension of the old South End on its way to Roxbury and Dorchester Neck (South Boston). The movement of low-income families in this direction was facilitated by the opening of the horse-car line from Scollay Sq. to Roxbury in 1856. The upshot of all this was that the City's attempt to establish the new South End as a posh neighborhood to compete with the Commonwealth's Back Bay venture failed almost as soon as it was initiated, and the elegant brownstones were converted to rooming houses in short order. The South End has remained a working-class neighborhood ever since. Though failing to control location, the intention to segregate residential sectors by class has been successful.

At the top of Telegraph Hill in South Boston, you get a fine view of the harbor and its islands. Castle Island has the most colorful history of the islands close to Boston. In 1665, Captain Davenport, commanding officer there at the time, was killed in his bed by a bolt of lightning. During the Revolutionary War, troops stationed at 'Castle William' saw little action and the fort was burned by the British during their retreat from Boston. Paul Revere was charged with refortifying the island. When Edgar Allan Poe enlisted in the army in 1827, he was sent to Castle Island to serve, and supposedly based 'The Cask of Amontillado' on a famous duel fought on the grounds ten years earlier. Finally, in 1891, the first bridge was built to the island and the fort was turned into a city park.

Thompson Island, directly south of Castle Island, is the site of the original Farm and Trade School for indigent boys. It was built in the 1830's, but by the 1840's a distinction was made between 'worthy' and 'delinquent' boys, and the latter were henceforth sent elsewhere. Ten thousand years of wind and waves have carved a huge cliff face in the drumlin on the northern end of the island, exposing its homogeneous contents of sand and gravel.

A little to the east of Thompson Island lies Spectacle Island, the site of Boston's first quarantining hospital (located there because of local protests over the earlier proposed site on Squantum Neck). In the mid-1880's, a series of summer hotels were built there, but were shortly thereafter raided and closed by the police because of their illegal forms of entertainment. It has since been used as a land-fill site, a police firing range, and fire department oil fire practice site.

Governors Island to the north (now obliterated by the airport) was the home of the first orchard in America. Apples, grapes, pears, and plums were grown there. Diminutive Apple Island, also consumed by airport expansion, was used for boxing matches in the late 1880's but seems to have proved too small for much else. Of Upper Middle and Lower Middle Ground, once half-tide shoals, there is no more. Upper Middle has apparently disappeared by natural erosion; Lower Middle, in the process of dredging the channel of Boston Harbor.

Castle Island

6   Directions

START		Intersection of BEACON ST. and MASSACHUSETTS AVE., Boston.
mi.	0.0	SOUTHEAST on MASSACHUSETTS AVE. (toward Boston)
	1.7	RIGHT onto HARRISON AVE.
	1.8	LEFT onto NORTHAMPTON ST.
	2.0	REJOIN MASSACHUSETTS AVE.
	2.3	LEFT onto T. A. GLYNN WAY
	2.4	RIGHT onto SOUTHAMPTON ST.
	3.0	LEFT onto DORCHESTER ST.
	3.4	RIGHT onto TELEGRAPH ST.
	3.8	RIGHT onto E. 6th ST.
	4.0	RIGHT onto H ST.
	4.1	LEFT onto COLUMBIA RD.
	4.2	RIGHT onto I ST., then CROSS W. J. DAY BLVD., then RIGHT onto BIKE PATH
	5.1	RIGHT onto causeway (circling Pleasure Bay) RIGHT on path (keeping Fort Independence to left)
	6.6	RIGHT onto W. J. DAY BLVD.
	7.2	RIGHT onto E. BROADWAY
	7.6	LEFT onto M ST.
	7.7	RIGHT onto E. 4th ST.
	7.9	HAIRPIN LEFT onto EMERSON ST.
	8.0	LEFT onto L ST.
	8.1	LEFT onto E. BROADWAY
	8.3	RIGHT onto EMERSON ST.
	8.6	LEFT onto DORCHESTER ST.
	8.7	RIGHT onto W. BROADWAY
	9.4	LEFT onto A ST.
	9.5	RIGHT onto W. 4th ST. (becomes E. BERKELEY ST. across bridge)
	10.3	BEAR RIGHT onto BERKELEY ST.
	10.9	LEFT onto BIKE PATH (center of COMMONWEALTH AVE.)
	11.6	RIGHT onto HEREFORD ST., then LEFT on COMMONWEALTH AVE.
	11.7	RIGHT onto MASSACHUSETTS AVE. to
	11.8	START.

A Back Bay mansion on Dartmouth Street

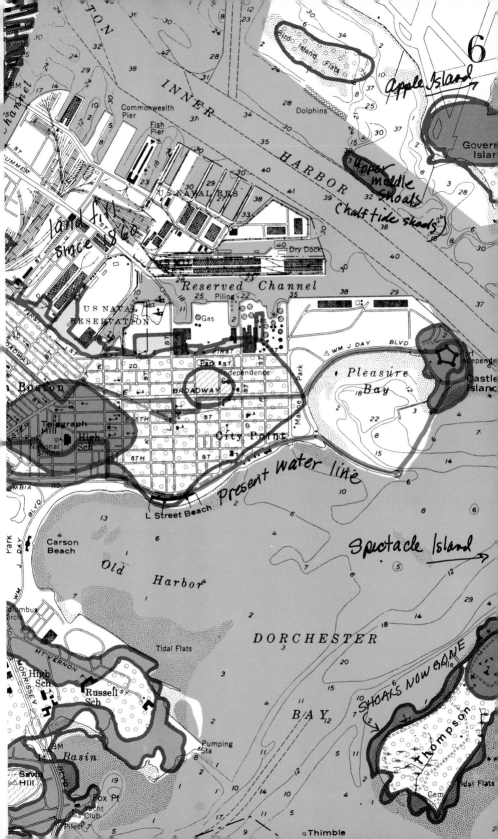

7 One If By Land

The Old Circumferential

Boston may be the 'hub,' but originally it had only one spoke connected firmly by land to the outlying wheel. This was fine for the maritime people who settled the Shawmut Peninsula in 1630 but it created difficulties 145 years later for anyone interested in the free flow of military intelligence. This ride, like the messengers of April 19, 1775, who wanted to make sure that somebody got through, follows both the 'land' and 'sea' routes which connected Boston with Cambridge at that time.

The Custom House seems like a good symbolic place to start this route even though Paul Revere made his way to the Charles River from the North End, that hotbed of political activism. Since the Charlestown Bridge was only first chartered by John Hancock a decade later, Revere rowed across after signaling for a horse to be waiting. The ferry, operated by Harvard for scholarship funds, wasn't available for special late night events. After landing on the Mishawum Peninsula, Revere rode straight up Main St. to the connection with the mainland and then headed for Cambridge. About halfway there, he spotted a roadblock, so he turned around and made his way to Lexington by way of Medford instead. He still arrived there a half hour ahead of William Dawes, who presumably had had to spend some time with his friends, the sentries at Boston Neck.

Revere, of course, rode right on by Charlestown Heights (Bunker and Breed's Hills), there being no monument to visit and, indeed, no reason to think that there might some day be one, since the battle of Bunker Hill was still two months off in the future. Between General Gage's spring offensive of 1775 and the British evacuation of Boston on

March 17, 1776, there were only two really impressive displays of military might, one for each of the hills overlooking Boston. The first was the battle of Bunker Hill (which actually took place on Breed's Hill, but all those drumlins look alike). The second one didn't occur until Washington upstaged General Howe's spring offensive of 1776 by fortifying Telegraph Hill in early March.

Most of the time between battles people were busy organizing. The various colonial factions at the Continental Congress in Philadelphia, for example, took until June 15, 1775, to decide to make Washington commander-in-chief of the various colonial forces that had been massing in Massachusetts since April 19. Washington arrived in Boston on July 3, a year and a day before Congress could agree to declare independence. He missed the battle of Bunker Hill, though he arrived in time for the debate over what the chain of command had been that day.

For the rest of the summer, Washington trained his troops to obey orders (too much democratic spirit) and bottled the British up in Boston. That is, he kept the British from coming out by land. The sea was open to them so they used it to call General Gage back to England to be replaced by General Howe, an old friend of Washington's. Like Boston cyclists today, Washington and Howe had begun waiting for spring by the end of November. Spring came earlier for Washington and, after taking Dorchester Heights, with a little patience, a few cannon balls, and an agreement not to bombard Howe anymore if he'd stop dragging his feet while hoping for reinforcements, Washington finally got him to depart from Boston, leaving the city free to prosper for the rest of the Revolutionary War.

Leaving Bunker Hill, this route proceeds around the old circumferential to Cambridge. The one section which Revere didn't travel that night the British did. For Dawes, who took the long way to Cambridge, the problem of crossing the Charles was relatively simple. After proceeding down Boston Neck toward Roxbury, he headed for the 'Great Bridge' built by Harvard in 1662. The boards, which were ripped up and hidden later on (forcing the British Regulars returning from Concord to go home by way of Charlestown), were still in place when he got there.

7   Directions

START	Intersection of INDIA ST. and STATE ST., Boston (Old Custom House to left).
mi. 0.0	WEST on STATE ST.
0.2	RIGHT onto CONGRESS ST.
0.3	RIGHT, then LEFT onto UNION ST. (at Dock Sq.)
0.5	LEFT onto HANOVER ST., then RIGHT onto CONGRESS ST.
0.6	CROSS NEW CHARDON ST. onto PORTLAND ST.
0.7	RIGHT onto CAUSEWAY ST.
1.0	LEFT across CHARLESTOWN BRIDGE
1.4	BEAR LEFT, then RIGHT onto PARK ST. (at end of bridge)
1.5	BEAR LEFT onto WARREN ST. (signs for Bunker Hill Monument)
1.7	RIGHT onto MONUMENT AVE.
1.8	LEFT onto HIGH ST. (Monument Sq.)
1.9	LEFT onto PLEASANT ST.
2.0	RIGHT onto WARREN ST.
2.2	STRAIGHT onto MAIN ST. (Thompson Sq.)
2.8	BEAR LEFT, then RIGHT (past Schrafft's) on MAIN ST., then LEFT (toward the roundhouse), then
3.0	BEAR LEFT onto CAMBRIDGE ST. (signs for Cambridge) (becomes WASHINGTON ST., Somerville, then KIRKLAND ST., Cambridge)
5.1	LEFT onto IRVING ST.
5.2	CROSS CAMBRIDGE ST. on IRVING ST. (*looks* like driveway)
5.4	RIGHT onto BROADWAY
5.5	LEFT onto WARE ST.
5.6	RIGHT onto HARVARD ST. (merges with MASSACHUSETTS AVE.)
5.7	BEAR LEFT (at Harvard Sq. kiosk) onto BRATTLE ST., then STRAIGHT across BOYLSTON ST. on BRATTLE ST.
5.8	BEAR LEFT onto ELLIOT ST. (Brattle St. forks right), then

CROSS MT. AUBURN ST. on ELLIOT ST.
6.0   RIGHT onto BOYLSTON ST. (becomes NORTH HARVARD ST., Brighton)
6.8   BEAR RIGHT onto FRANKLIN ST.
7.2   CROSS LINCOLN ST., then
LEFT along SIDEWALK and over BRIDGE
7.3   RIGHT onto CAMBRIDGE ST.
7.4   LEFT onto HARVARD ST.
9.7   LEFT onto BOYLSTON ST. (becomes HUNTINGTON AVE., Jamaica Plain)
10.4   BEAR RIGHT onto TREMONT ST.
10.9   RIGHT onto COLUMBUS AVE. (under bridge at Roxbury Crossing), then
11.0   LEFT onto ROXBURY ST.
11.3   BEAR LEFT onto DUDLEY ST.
11.6   LEFT onto WARREN ST.
11.8   BEAR RIGHT onto WASHINGTON ST.
14.1   RIGHT onto WATER ST.
14.2   LEFT onto HAWES ST.
14.3   LEFT onto KILBY ST.
14.4   RIGHT onto DOANE ST.
14.5   RIGHT onto BROAD ST., then
LEFT onto CENTRAL ST., then
CROSS INDIA ST. and circle Old Custom House to
14.6   START.

Bunker Hill Monument, Charlestown

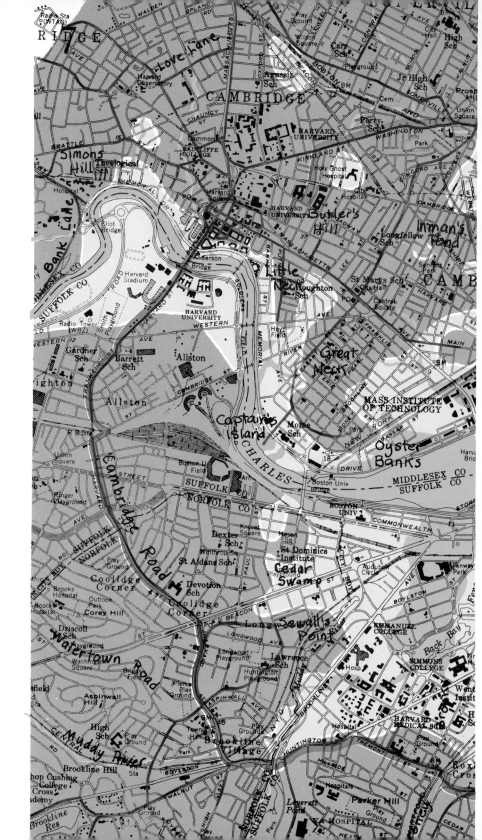

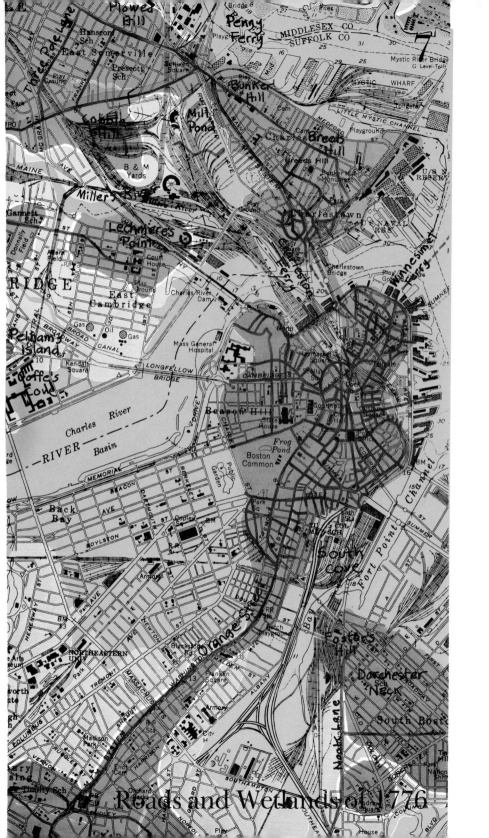

Roads and Wetlands of 1776

Section 2

8 Gateways to the North

Medford–Malden–Charlestown

The rule of 'You cut and I'll choose' is one of mankind's oldest and most useful. It is the archetypical compromise, and compromise, if it does not in fact make the world go round, makes it possible to get through the day. For all its usefulness, however, there are circumstances in which the rule of 'You cut and I'll choose' may not be applied. The history of the area covered in this ride is a catalogue of cases in which it didn't.

When Governor Winthrop arrived in the Massachusetts Bay Colony, he had to find a place where everybody in his party would be willing to live together. Some wanted to live along the Mystic River and others wanted to live along the Charles. A compromise was tried: the group could live in Charlestown and have the best, or at least *some,* of both worlds. The idea was soon abandoned, and the settlement broke into smaller groups who went to live in Boston, along the Charles and along the Mystic, having largely both cut and chosen for the previous inhabitants of those areas, the Indians.

The settlers who didn't cut and run set up shop in Charlestown, which in those days (the early 1600's) included, besides present-day Charlestown, Somerville, some of Medford, Everett, Malden, Melrose, and Stoneham. Those who chose Charlestown counted among its assets its location as a gateway to the North across the Mystic. The Penny Ferry was established in 1640 and ran between Charlestown Neck and present-day Everett. Medford at this time offered the other crossing place over the Mystic, this at Medford Square. Teamsters and travelers chose where to cross, and the towns of Charlestown and Medford took their cut. Sullivan Sq. and Medford Sq. remain to this day major crossing points for the Mystic in all manners of conveyance.

8

In 1649, Malden was set off from Charlestown. What this amounted to was the legal acknowledgment of a long obvious division between Charlestown proper and 'Mystic-side.' (The division from a legal point of view turned out to be somewhat less simple, for Charlestown took great pains to hold onto one critical piece of land north of the Mystic: Stoneham, in which Spot Pond is located.) Malden fell naturally into three parts: a very wet portion to the south, a middle portion (through which the Northern Boundary Fault runs on its way from Medford to Saugus), and, to the north, 'an uncouth wilderness.' Whether the subsequent political divisions roughly corresponding to these natural ones fell or were pushed is a matter of some debate.

The 'uncouth wilderness' served as a common ground for the citizens of Malden, everyone being allowed to use it for grazing and timber. As its value became more clear, the town decided to avoid any future squabbles about the use of the land by cutting it up and fairly distributing it among the citizenry. In 1849, Melrose became a separate town from Malden. Since there was only one good road between Malden proper and the former common ground, and this was a through road to Stoneham and other points north, the cutting and choosing which resulted in Melrose was relatively straightforward.

Everett's subsequent parting of the way with Malden was not so happy. Malden, Melrose, and Medford, not having sufficient fresh water supplies within their boundaries to meet their needs, jointly purchased the franchise of the Spot Pond Water Company in 1869. South Malden, having always felt like the third sibling who shows up after the others have happily cut and chosen, was most unhappy about the water arrangements, wishing no part of the considerable expense involved in bringing the fresh water in. Everett became a separate town in 1870, though as a consequence, it was ultimately obliged to go to Charlestown to augment *its* meager supplies of fresh water, for Medford, Malden, and Melrose would not agree to cut up Spot Pond any further, giving Everett no choice in the matter.

8 Directions

START	MEDFORD SQUARE, Medford.
mi. 0.0	SOUTHEAST on RIVERSIDE AVE.
0.5	LEFT onto PLEASANT ST.
0.7	LEFT onto PARK ST., then
	RIGHT onto MAGOUN ST.
1.1	LEFT onto SPRING ST.
1.3	RIGHT onto CENTRAL AVE. (becomes MEDFORD ST., Malden)
2.0	LEFT onto HIGHLAND AVE.
2.7	RIGHT onto ELM ST.
3.0	LEFT onto PLEASANT ST.
3.1	RIGHT onto COMMERCIAL ST.
3.3	LEFT onto EXCHANGE ST.
3.5	LEFT onto MAIN ST.
3.6	LEFT onto PLEASANT ST.
3.7	RIGHT onto WASHINGTON ST.
3.8	LEFT onto FLORENCE ST.
4.0	STRAIGHT onto COMMERCIAL ST.
4.4	LEFT onto CHARLES ST.
4.5	RIGHT onto CANAL ST.
4.9	LEFT onto MEDFORD ST.
5.2	RIGHT onto MAIN ST.
6.1	SECOND RIGHT off ROTARY onto BROADWAY (becomes ALFORD ST., Charlestown)
7.5	RIGHT onto MAIN ST. (becomes MYSTIC AVE., Somerville)
8.3	BEAR LEFT following signs for McGrath Highway on MYSTIC ST.
8.8	RIGHT onto SHORE DR.
8.9	LEFT onto BIKE PATH
9.8	WALK across HARVARD ST. and LEFT over BRIDGE
9.9	LEFT onto STADIUM ACCESS RD.
10.0	LEFT at stadium, then
	RIGHT onto BIKE PATH
10.5	LEFT onto RIVERSIDE DR.
11.0	RIGHT at CITY HALL MALL
11.1	LEFT onto SALEM ST. to
11.2	START.

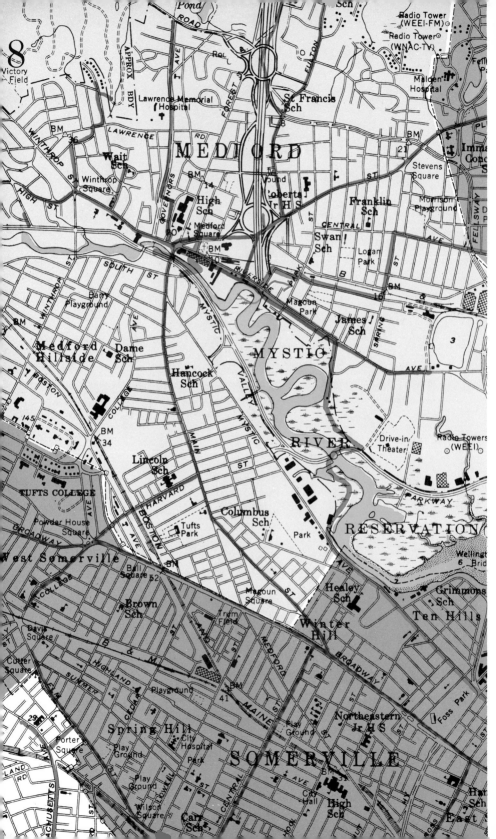

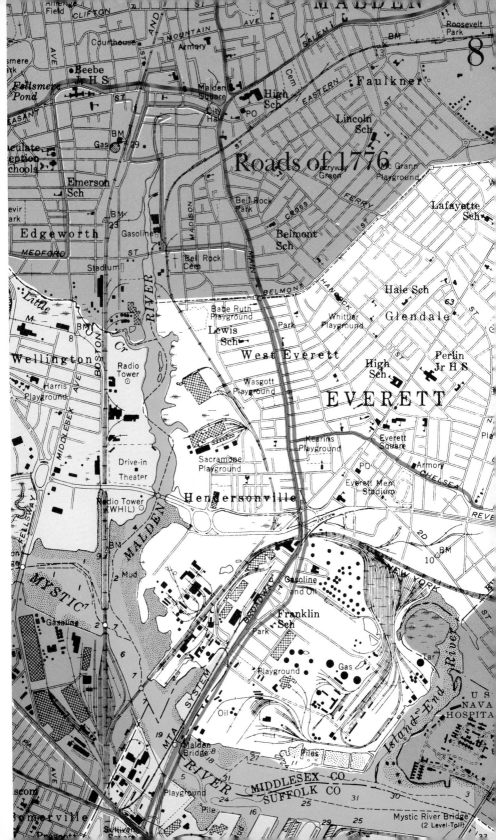

9 The Iron Rhomboid

Malden–Saugus–Melrose

The name 'Saugus,' like the land which it originally designated, comes to us from the Pawtucket Indians. That the Pawtucket Indians and their English neighbors were both uneasy about the transfer of dominion over this land, which stretched from Salem to Boston, was suggested by Cotton Mather in 1632: 'The indians began to be quarrelsome touching the Bounds of Land which they had sold to the English, but God ended the controversy by sending Smallpox among the Indians at Saugust, who were before that time exceeding numerous.' In 1637 a piece of legislation exemplary in its terseness was enacted: 'Saugust is called Lin.' Present-day Saugus got its name back when it was set off from Lynn as a separate town in 1815.

Malden and Melrose, like all the other towns with English names which surround Saugus, were, of course, also at one time Indian lands which were acquired by the early British settlers. From the advent of the British to the beginning of the nineteenth century, however, Malden–Melrose and Saugus had rather different histories. For one thing, Saugus got an earlier start as a place to live and work than Malden–Melrose, first by being right on the ocean and second by using its river to run a series of water-powered industries.

The Saugus Iron Works opened in the 1640's. This was the first iron works in the hemisphere and it had all the apparent earmarks of a big success. It had solid financial backing from England, and a ready supply of skilled and unskilled workers, including not a few Scottish prisoners of war who came to work off their time in the Colony rather than cool their heels in jail at home. It also had an ideal location. Iron ore had been found in the marshes around Saugus, gabbro (for flux) could be had from nearby Nahant, there were vast reaches of forest just out in the back yard which could be felled and burned to make the charcoal to fuel the furnaces, and there was water, both for power and for shipping the finished product out. The water came from the Saugus River, which flows from the uplands down over the Northern Boundary Fault in Saugus and then into the ocean.

The Saugus Iron Works was relatively short-lived, partly because it was grossly mismanaged and partly because it soon ran through its local supplies of timber and iron ore. In 1722, a new mill was built slightly upriver from the already defunct Iron Works. This mill did well for a while grinding corn but eventually it too went downhill. In 1792, the mill was purchased by the enterprising George Makepeace, who refurbished it and added a couple of snuff-mortars, making Saugus the snuff capital of the region and Mr. Makepeace a very wealthy mill-owner. He soon added facilities for grinding chocolate and making more money.

Malden–Melrose, once it graduated from being 'the other side of the Mystic' and part of Charlestown to 'gateway to the North' (if you were going north), was on its way, though it remained small in population until the Odiorne family took it upon themselves to start a company to manufacture nails. Their success and the handiness to all sorts of transportation north and south encouraged other companies to do likewise, and Malden–Melrose was in business as Saugus had long been.

9 Directions

START	MALDEN SQUARE, Malden.
mi. 0.0	NORTH on MAIN ST.
0.9	RIGHT into PINE BANKS PARK
1.0	RIGHT at FIRST FORK
1.4	LEFT at FORK
1.5	RIGHT onto MAIN ST.
2.4	RIGHT onto UPHAM ST. (becomes ESSEX ST., Saugus)
4.8	LEFT onto VINE ST. (just after Rte. 1 bridge)
5.5	RIGHT onto MAIN ST.
5.8	LEFT onto SUMMER ST.
6.0	RIGHT onto PLEASANT ST.
6.2	RIGHT onto CENTRAL ST.
6.4	STRAIGHT (around statue) on CENTRAL ST.
7.5	RIGHT onto LINCOLN AVE.
7.8	LEFT on LINCOLN AVE.
9.1	BEAR RIGHT onto LAWRENCE ST.
9.4	RIGHT onto BEACH ST.
9.6	LEFT onto SALEM ST. to
11.6	START.

Saugus Iron Works: a reconstruction of the original 17th-century complex

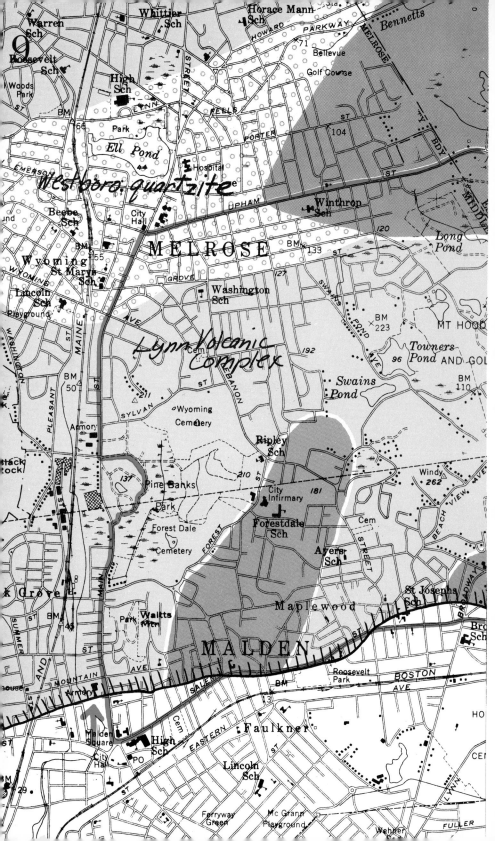

Westboro quartzite

MELROSE

Lynn Volcanic Complex

MALDEN

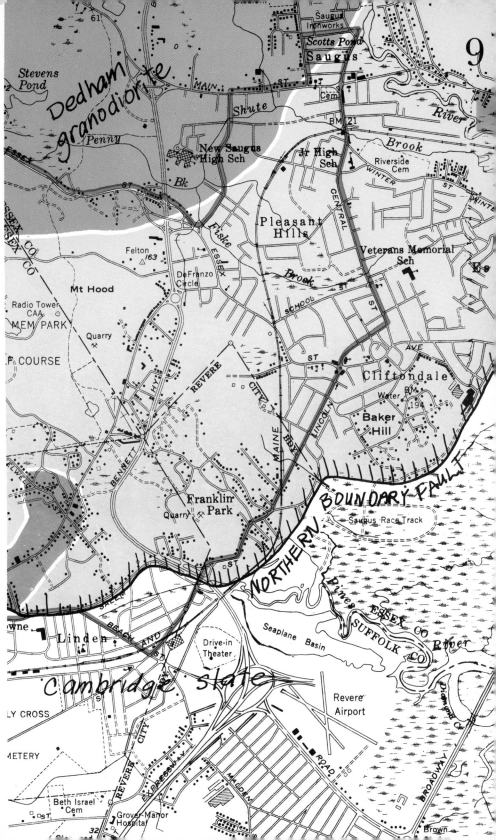

10 The Saugus Salt Marsh

The southern end of this ride loops around City Hall in Revere, the modest birthplace of Horatio Alger. The northwest corner of this town illustrates three land uses characteristic of recently made land: drive-in theaters, shopping centers, and airports. (The shopping center on the eastern side of the expressway has replaced a small general aviation airport. A seaplane landing basin lies to the north.)

As you cross under Route 1, a large quarry will come into view on your left, providing an opportunity for intimate examination of the cliff face visible in intermittent glimpses for the last half mile. This is the surface of the great Northern Boundary Fault, a titanic slippage in the earth's crust which raised the northern portion of the Boston metropolitan area some 300 million years ago. The bedrock south of the fault, underlying the Saugus swamp, is Cambridge slate; but above the fault in this region are the various felsites of the Lynn volcanic complex.

As you turn away from the fault and head down the access road off Marshall St., you may run into slight difficulty. After any moderate to heavy rainstorm, this road becomes a streambed and you'll be obliged to walk (or carry) your bike across it. Even in dry weather, some walking may be required, as the road is unpaved for a short section. You can always take Lincoln Ave. around the other side of Baker Hill instead, of course, but we think that the dirt road section is worth the effort. Since the stream takes to the road only some of the time, erosion patterns in the road (streambed), formation of ripple marks and 'braided channels' in the sand, the occurrence of 'stream piracy' in miniature, natural grading of the particles carried by water, and other hydrodynamic specialties are displayed most beautifully when road conditions are worst (or shortly thereafter).

Urban wetland areas such as the Saugus swamp often invite particular uses of land not provided for elsewhere in the community. The term 'wetland' is used here in its technical sense of 'poorly drained soil' and does not necessarily imply the presence of surface water. The term 'wasteland' is a more popular, though not altogether appropriate, label. Informal uses of such areas typically include illegal dumping of trash and other recreational activities which are incompatible with either parks or residential areas (such as flying model airplanes, drinking alcoholic beverages, building campfires, riding trail bikes, and so on). More formally planned intrusions into urban wetlands are the siting of radio towers, electric power and telephone lines, unpaved racetracks, and paved highways. All of these uses are facilitated by the low purchase price and relatively low esteem in which 'wastelands' are held by the community.

The chief difference between undisturbed wetlands and those which have been interfered with by man is that the latter generally have reduced ecological value. The total productivity (support of abundant food-producing organisms) and the capacity to filter pollutants and to reduce flooding are impaired when the flow of water is either blocked (forming stagnant pools) or greatly increased by channelization (concentrating the force of storm-water runoff), or when burdened with too heavy loads of organic or toxic material. Nevertheless, except for those for whom aesthetics and purity are inseparable, the *recreational* value of such wetland areas need not be diminished by disturbance.

The climb along the side of Baker Hill (also on 'bad' road) brings you partway up the side of the Northern Boundary Fault through an area which some might think of as 'wasteland' but which supports a fairly interesting range of plants and good wildlife cover. The mixture of open spaces and dense clusters of shrubs and trees provides both food and hiding places for small birds and mammals. Wild cherry trees, staghorn sumac, and rose hips are feature attractions for animals, human and nonhuman alike, in late summer.

10 The sudden appearance of wild mushrooms after heavy rains also compensates the traveler adventurous enough to ford the shallow stream and leap a few puddles along the way.

The eastern section of this ride takes in Lynn, home of Lydia Pinkham's pioneering patent medicine factory and notable for its gazebo on the common and the salty, breezy Salem Turnpike, one of the few turnpike-era turnpikes that always showed a profit. If you didn't pick up lunch in Revere or Lynn, by the way, don't despair midway between the crossings of the Saugus and Pines Rivers, for although there are only two buildings on the entire stretch, one of them is a snack bar.

Saugus Dump: finding a use for wetland

10 Directions

START	MARKET SQUARE, Lynn.
mi. 0.0	WEST on COMMON ST.
0.1	LEFT onto WESTERN AVE. (becomes SALEM TURNPIKE, Saugus; becomes BROADWAY, Revere)
3.7	AROUND ROTARY on BROADWAY
5.0	LEFT onto BEACH ST.
5.4	STRAIGHT onto SCHOOL ST. (Beach St. forks right)
5.8	BEAR RIGHT on SCHOOL ST. (DiPesa Sq.)
6.0	RIGHT onto BROADWAY, then LEFT onto REVERE ST., then
6.1	BEAR RIGHT onto MALDEN ST.
7.1	RIGHT onto WASHINGTON ST.
7.5	CROSS ROUTE 60 onto WESLEY ST.
7.6	BEAR RIGHT onto LYNN ST.
7.9	RIGHT onto SALEM ST. (under Rte. 1)
8.4	RIGHT onto MARSHALL ST. (over railroad bridge) (becomes PARK ST., Saugus)
8.6	RIGHT onto SAUGUS RACETRACK ACCESS RD. (dirt road)
8.9	RIGHT around RACETRACK
10.0	EXIT RACETRACK RIGHT onto SAUGUS AVE. EXTENSION
10.4	STRAIGHT on SAUGUS AVE. (pavement resumes)
10.8	RIGHT onto LINCOLN AVE. (becomes BOSTON ST., Lynn)
11.6	BEAR RIGHT on BOSTON ST. (just after river)
12.8	RIGHT onto MARION ST.
12.9	RIGHT onto CENTRE ST. to
13.2	START.

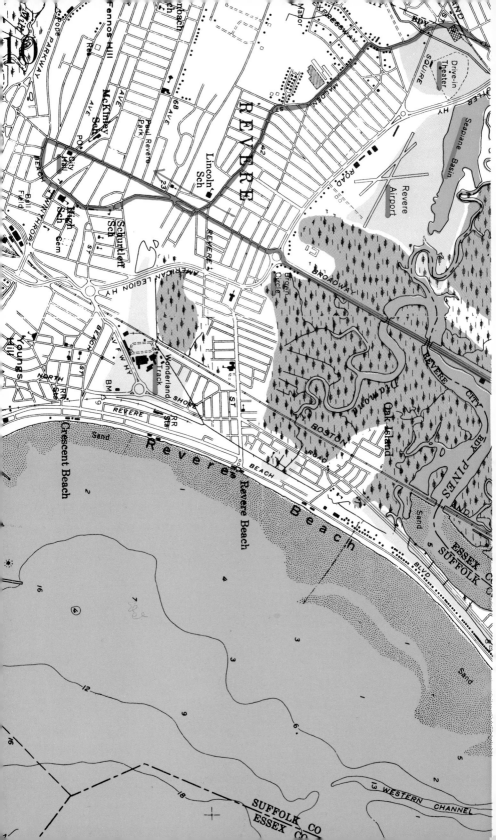

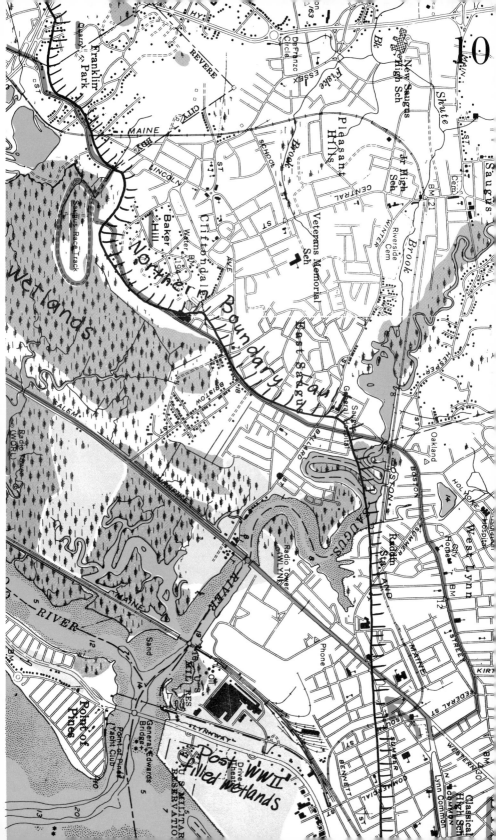

11   Chelsea Drumlins

Chelsea is where you go if you'd rather be in Boston but came along after Boston was full. Like an eddy in the urban stream, Chelsea collects things: hospitals, military facilities, factories, boxcars, sailors, et cetera. The area covered by this ride is made up of urban flatland along the shores of the Mystic and Chelsea rivers and a series of abrupt hills, all of which are piles of gravel left behind by the glacier some ten thousand years ago. Such hills are called 'drumlins' and are one of the most interesting, annoying, amusing, and important physical features of the entire Boston Basin. Bunker Hill, Breed's Hill, Beacon Hill, Telegraph Hill, and Castle Island are all drumlins. In fact, almost all of the hills in the Basin are drumlins and, without them, the history and development of Boston and environs would have taken a very different course. Roads were bent around them, forts were put on top of them, and some of the best views of Boston await those who puff and pant their way to the summits of them.

Drumlins generally seem to occur in swarms or herds, Boston having almost two hundred of them in an area less than fifteen miles wide. Locally, they are confined almost without exception to the land lying between the Northern and Southern Boundary Faults, where most glacial deposits accumulated. Drumlins tend to be under two hundred feet high and about half a mile long. They are usually oval in shape with the long axis parallel to the direction of the movement of the advancing ice (southeasterly). The end toward the glacier is often short and steep while the other tapers gradually.

The exact reason for the occurrence of drumlins is still

fairly mysterious, though geologists conjecture that they may have begun as morainal ridges. These are piles of rock and debris caught up in the ice and then dropped at the edge of the melting glacier, accumulating in one place if the ice melts at the same rate at which it pushes forward. If the ice melted back leaving a moraine but then, due to a new drop in temperature, advanced again, it could ram into its own disposal site, breaking the moraine into small pieces and spreading them over the landscape.

As hills, drumlins encourage particular uses of land that seem unrelated but in fact have a good deal in common. The most annoying aspect of a drumlin (or any other steep-sided hill) is also the feature which most determines the use of its land. Steep slopes mean a long climb and no water at the top: a poor site for houses and stores (unless all the other land has been used up), but good for pastures, orchards, and forts. The last areas of a city to be developed are the very high ground and the very low (wet) ground. The low, flat ground (once filled) gets cars, trucks, trains, and planes; while the high and dry tends to get facilities characterized by the need for a lot of land but limited comings and goings, such as hospitals, rest homes, seminaries, military bases. There are eighteen drumlins on the map for this ride (though you only have to climb two of them). Orient Heights is a real showpiece drumlin, clearly visible as you come down the end of Mt. Bellingham.

11 Directions

START	SULLIVAN SQUARE, Charlestown.
mi. 0.0	NORTH on ALFORD ST. (becomes BROADWAY, Everett)
0.8	BEAR RIGHT onto BOW ST.
1.1	RIGHT onto BEACHAM ST.
1.5	BEAR RIGHT onto BEHEN ST.
1.8	LEFT onto MARKET ST. (parallel to Island End River)
2.0	RIGHT onto BEACHAM ST.
2.3	BEAR RIGHT onto WILLIAMS ST.
2.9	LEFT onto PEARL ST.
3.1	RIGHT onto PARK ST.
3.4	RIGHT onto BELLINGHAM ST.
4.0	LEFT onto EASTERN AVE.
4.6	RIGHT onto CRESCENT AVE. (first right after railroad tracks)
5.0	LEFT onto CLINTON ST.
5.4	RIGHT onto BROADWAY
5.8	RIGHT onto BEACH ST.
6.0	LEFT onto WINTHROP AVE.
6.2	LEFT onto BROADWAY
6.8	BEAR RIGHT on BROADWAY
6.9	RIGHT onto STOCKTON ST.
7.0	LEFT onto CLARK AVE.
7.1	RIGHT onto CREST AVE.
7.2	LEFT onto HILLSIDE AVE.
7.5	LEFT onto SUMMIT AVE.
7.7	LEFT into park path loop
7.8	LEFT onto SUMMIT AVE.
7.9	LEFT onto WARREN AVE., then RIGHT onto FRANKLIN AVE.
8.0	LEFT onto JEFFERSON AVE.
8.1	RIGHT onto WASHINGTON AVE.
8.2	RIGHT on WASHINGTON AVE.
8.4	LEFT onto NICHOLS ST.
9.0	LEFT onto FERRY ST.
9.3	RIGHT onto CHELSEA ST.
9.8	HARD LEFT onto BROADWAY
10.1	THIRD RIGHT off ROTARY on

BROADWAY (becomes ALFORD ST., Charlestown)

11

11.7 RIGHT around ROTARY to

12.0 START.

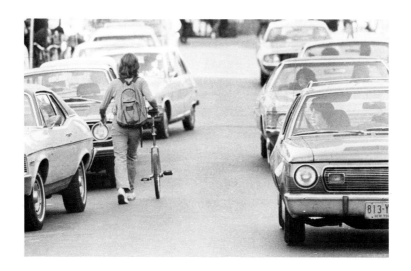

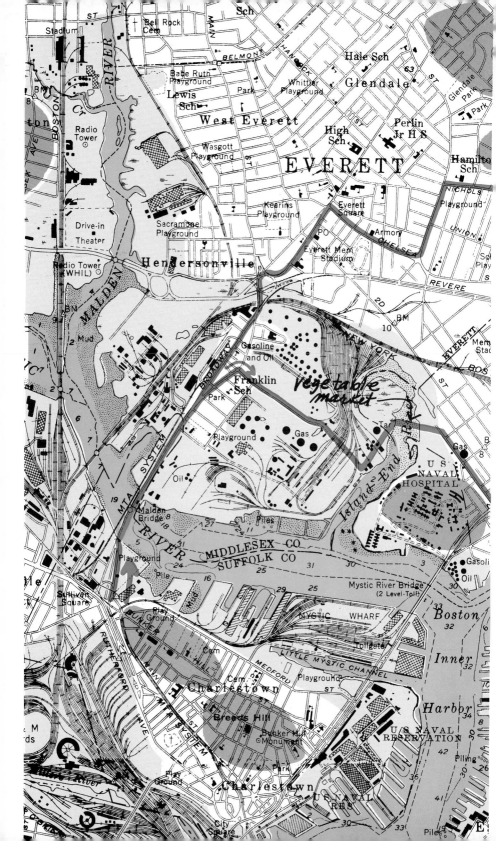

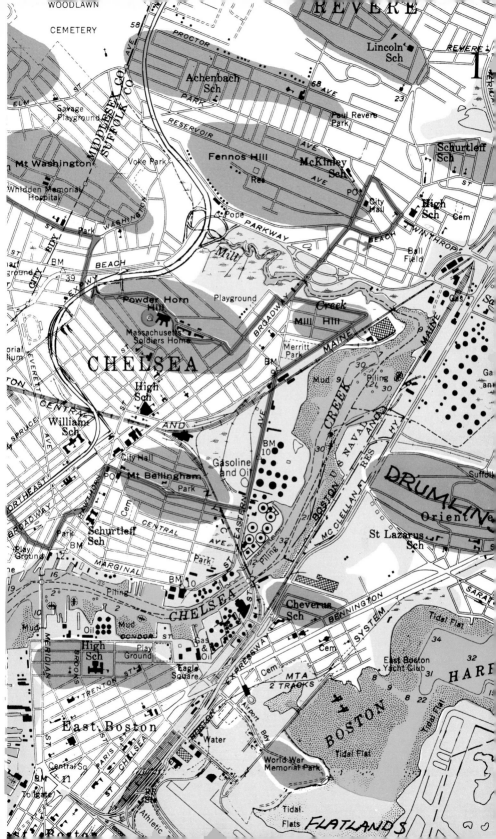

12 The Long Arm

East Boston–Winthrop

In this ride, the drumlins encountered in Chelsea solemnly march into the sea. (The underlying slate is tilted down toward the water, as elsewhere in the Basin.) Some of these hills have been partially eroded at their seaward ends (Cottage Hill/Winthrop Head), while others remain almost intact, showing the classic drumlin shape: steep on the northwest side, sloping gently to the southeast (Orient Heights, Deer Island). Some (the beautiful Wood Island and Governors Island) have been swallowed up entirely by the expanding airport.

Cottage Hill and Orient Heights both afford excellent views, should the rider wish to deviate slightly from the route. Deer Island is seen at its best from Cottage Hill. Classic in its shape and its allotment to public use, Deer Island has almost no trees and few buildings, being occupied jointly by a jail, a sewage plant, and a military installation. From Orient Heights, you can see all of Boston and the harbor islands.

The beaches in Revere and Winthrop have been formed in large part from material eroded from the drumlins, a process that is still going on. Shirley Gut, entirely filled in by sediment by 1936, was deep enough for a man-o'-war to slip through to capture a British powder ship in the War of 1812. A side trip to Point Shirley, though again not on the itinerary, is recommended for those with the time. Nowhere more than at the causeway to Deer Island is the sense of being Away more vivid. The island looks (deliberately) forbidding, though according to one of its former residents they averaged a hundred escapes from the jail a year at the time of his stay. The town of Winthrop is so far out that a private, non-MBTA bus line carries people out to Point Shirley, though one can see the landmark towers of Boston from there with no difficulty. The fact that a lot of the houses are shuttered after Labor Day only adds to the aura of the surreal.

Sheltered in among the drumlins is Belle Isle Marsh, bounded in East Boston by the V of Saratoga and Bennington Streets (which form a nice Front Street–Back Street pair farther down into East Boston). Note the MBTA car-barns. All the cars on the East Boston–Revere ('Blue') Line are equipped with overhead trolley brackets in addition to third-rail contact runners, for the third rail ends and the overhead wire begins under Maverick Square. Belle Isle Marsh, although threatened by the Winthrop dump to the east and Logan Airport to the south, holds up pretty well. It is the in-town counterpart to the marshes of Saugus. Attempts to build a high-speed road through it have, so far, been successfully repulsed by the residents of East Boston.

Unfortunately, Belle Isle Marsh is one of the worst areas of noise pollution from aircraft using Logan Airport. It can be literally deafening. The second major noise fan is over Eagle Hill, one of the most densely populated regions of East Boston. Other ways in which the people of East Boston are encroached upon: the old story of river frontage going for oil tanks (Condor St.), the havoc wrought in local vehicular and pedestrian traffic by the Sumner and Callahan Tunnels (Central Sq.), and the proposed conversion of the waterfront facing Boston to a containerized freight terminal.

12 Directions

START	MAVERICK SQUARE, East Boston.
mi. 0.0	SOUTHWEST at MAVERICK SQ.
0.1	LEFT onto SUMNER ST.
0.7	LEFT onto JEFFRIES ST.
0.8	LEFT onto MAVERICK ST.
1.2	RIGHT onto CHELSEA ST.
2.1	RIGHT onto BENNINGTON ST.
4.5	RIGHT onto WINTHROP AVE.
5.1	RIGHT onto WINTHROP PARKWAY (becomes REVERE ST., Winthrop)
5.4	BEAR RIGHT onto CREST AVE.
6.0	RIGHT onto WINTHROP SHORE DR.
7.0	RIGHT onto BEACON ST.
7.3	RIGHT onto SHIRLEY ST.
7.5	LEFT onto WASHINGTON AVE.
8.1	RIGHT onto WINTHROP ST.
8.5	STRAIGHT onto HERMON ST. (at Winthrop Sq.)
8.8	LEFT onto MAIN ST. (becomes SARATOGA ST., East Boston)
10.0	STRAIGHT, then BEAR LEFT on SARATOGA ST.
11.2	RIGHT, then LEFT across Eagle Sq. onto EAGLE ST.
11.4	RIGHT onto CONDOR ST.
12.0	LEFT onto MERIDAN ST. to
13.0	START.

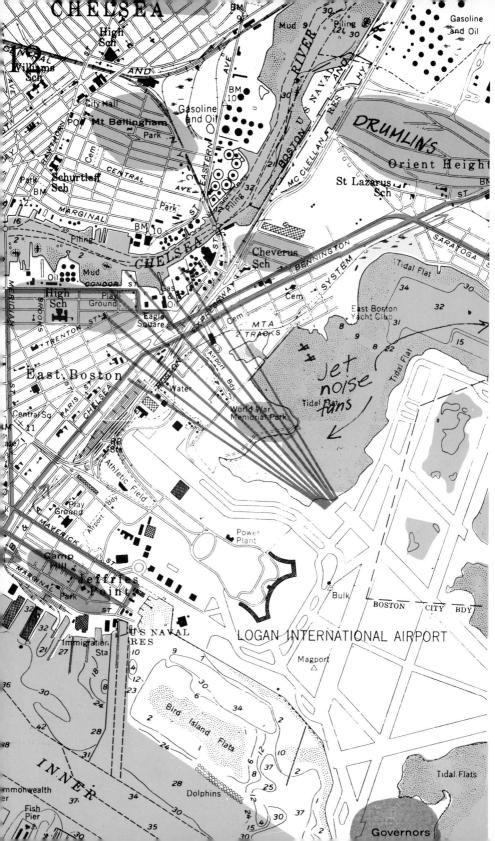

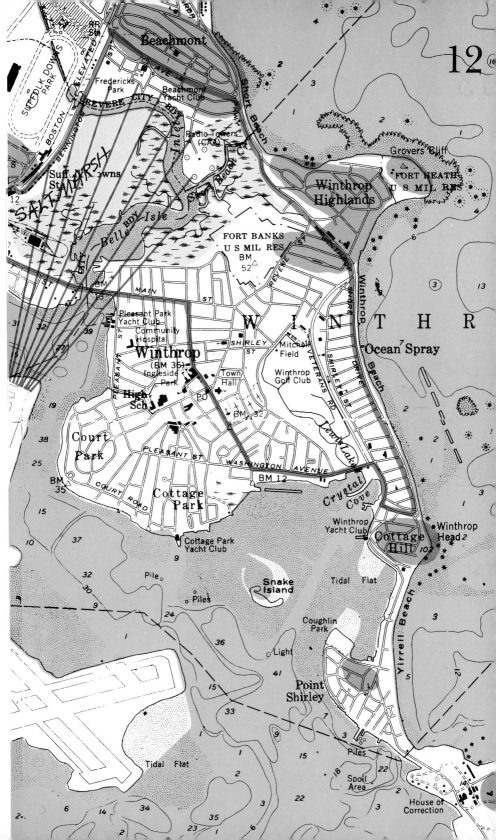

13　Somerville Squares

This route offers a broad sampling of intersections which are irregular enough to merit being called 'squares' (sic) by Bostonians. (The one or two clear-cut right-angle turns which occur on this route do not do so in any of the sixteen squares through which you will pass.) A glance at the 1830 road map shows that most squares are to be found at the intersections of roads already existing then. Turnpike construction, the latest fad in through-road building, was just giving way to railroad construction. By the time modern 'thruways' began to replace railroads, all the spaces between the old main roads had been filled by short residential streets. This 'residential filler' made many squares more complicated than before, but it also forced thruway builders to go elsewhere. The few squares formed by the intersection of short, post-1830 roads all happen to be 'honorary squares' whose names you probably couldn't find on any map but this one.

'True squares' (roughly, squares whose names *do* show up on normal street maps) are basically intersections of through roads. As the foci of the street network, 'true squares' tend to have well-known names partly because they are places where critical route decisions are made. They are also places through which relatively many people pass, so they tend to be centers of commercial and governmental activity, another good reason for naming them. This route has 'true squares' ranging in their transportational and commercial importance from the bustling Medford and Porter Squares to the unobtrusive Ball Sq. Powderhouse Sq. gives an idea of past uses of central places. The seventeenth-century grist mill there was converted to a powderhouse before the Revolutionary War. Unfortunately for the revolutionaries, this central location was just as convenient for the British (who marched out and confiscated the powder stored there) as it was for them.

When pared down to their 1830 simplicity, squares are not only easier to find on the map, but the reasons for their being where they are also show up a little better. Going north out of Boston, the bridges over the Charles River concentrate traffic at a limited set of points. To get from any such point to where you are going involves a series of decisions as to which prongs to take in a series of 'Y squares' which fan out to fill up the expanding circle. Travel is not, of course, limited to just to and from Boston, so all along the way there are more fan centers. Somerville, with Sullivan Sq. (Charlestown), Kendall Sq. (East Cambridge), and Harvard Sq. (West Cambridge) to the south, Medford Sq. to the north, and Powderhouse Sq. to the west, has many 'X squares' which are formed by the intersection of major and minor fans, making it an ideal place to go square sampling.

Sampling squares also happens to be a good way to sample fire stations. There is no neat one-to-one relationship between firehouses and squares, of course, but they do go together frequently. The reason is clear: squares are in the middle of all the best routes to the 'residential filler' streets. All fire stations are interesting but our favorite is the one at Inman Sq.

13 Directions

START   Intersection of HIGH ST. and MAIN ST., Medford.

mi. 0.0   NORTHWEST on HIGH ST. (Medford Sq.)

0.5   LEFT onto WINTHROP ST. (no sign, Winthrop Sq.)

0.8   RIGHT onto WEST ST. (just beyond McLaughlin Sq.)

1.1   STRAIGHT onto NORTH ST. (Leahy Sq.)

2.0   LEFT onto BROADWAY

2.3   RIGHT onto HOLLAND ST. (Teele Sq.)

2.9   STRAIGHT onto ELM ST. (Davis Sq.)

3.1   STRAIGHT on ELM ST. (Cutter Sq.)

3.8   LEFT onto SOMERVILLE AVE. (Wilson Sq.)

4.7   STRAIGHT on SOMERVILLE AVE. (Gerrior Sq.)

4.8   RIGHT onto WEBSTER AVE. (Union Sq.)

4.9   RIGHT onto NEWTON ST. (B&M railroad bridge)

5.0   STRAIGHT onto CONCORD ST. (Concord Sq.) then
LEFT onto SPRINGFIELD ST. (far end of Concord Sq.)

5.3   RIGHT onto BEACON ST. (Inman or Calnan Sq.)

6.3   BEAR RIGHT over B&M railroad bridge then immediately
LEFT onto SOMERVILLE AVE.

6.6   RIGHT onto MASS. AVE. (Porter Sq.)

7.1   RIGHT onto DAY ST.

7.3   STRAIGHT onto COLLEGE AVE. (Davis Sq.)

7.8   RIGHT onto BROADWAY (first right in Powderhouse Sq.)

7.9   LEFT onto BOSTON AVE. (Ball Sq.)

8.6   RIGHT onto COLLEGE ST. (over B&M railroad bridge)

9.0   RIGHT onto GEORGE ST. (sign for Royall House)

9.1   LEFT onto MAIN ST.

9.3   STRAIGHT on MAIN ST. (Cavanaugh Sq.)   13
       to
9.6   START.

Inman Square Fire Station

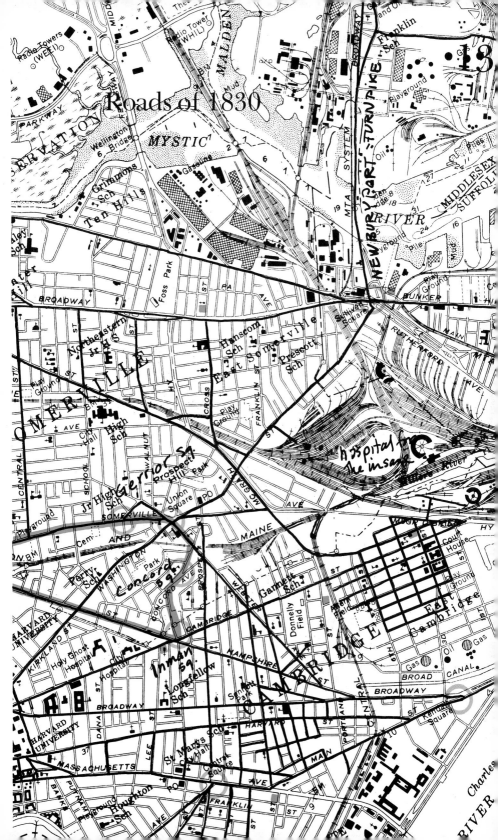

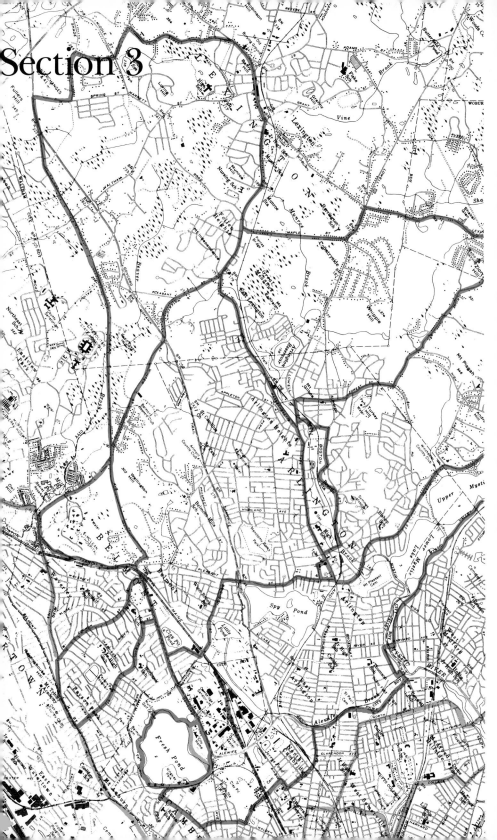

Section 3

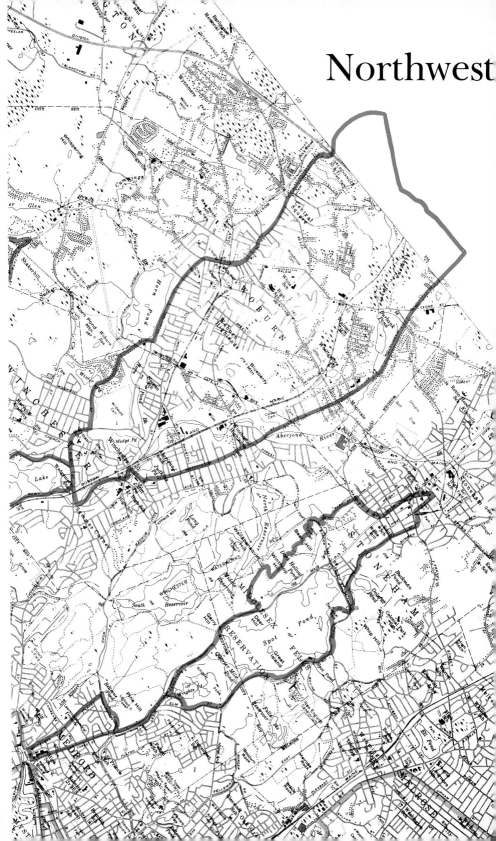

14 Belmont

Inside and Out

This ride samples two quite distinct regions: *inside* the Boston Basin and *outside* the Boston Basin. Belmont is a good place to do this, because it's one of the few places where the edge of the *topographical* Basin (bounded by the Fells Uplands to the north, the Needham Uplands to the west, and the Blue Hills to the south) coincides exactly with the edge of the *geological* Basin. The latter is defined by cracks in the bedrock, referred to as the Northern Boundary Fault, the Mother Brook Fault, and the Southern Boundary Fault, where bedrock formed since the beginning of the Appalachian Revolution is met by the mostly older rocks which surround the Basin.

Sometime during this great geological 'revolution,' the bedrock outside the area defined by these faults was shoved up and slightly over the land in between (like squeezing a soft-center chocolate) accentuating the basin-like shape of the region. (Since the bedrock tilts downward beneath the sea, little is known of its eastern end.) The long mountain-building period began 500 million years ago and lasted more than 200 million years. During that time, tremendous pressure (possibly the result of a collision between the drifting continents of North America and Europe) folded, tore, bent, and generally mutilated the earth's crust along the whole of the East Coast, forming the entire Appalachian mountain chain, as well as the many faults which now complicate our bedrock map.

The contours of the uplands and the Basin have been much softened by erosion over the years, as has the great mountain range beyond. The only major changes in the landscape since that time resulted when the continents split apart again (leaving the Continental Shelf), and when a visit by a continental ice sheet shaped the surface features of the land as we know it today. Actually, New England has welcomed several glaciers at one time or another. The most recent, about ten thousand years ago, came to the Boston area from the northwest, scraping the bedrock as it advanced, and carrying some of the scrapings over the edge of the faults into the Basin. As the great ice sheet finally retreated, melt-water streams carried a further load of rubble down into the lowlands. Residual blocks of ice clogged the valleys and the harbor; and the general disarray caused by piles of sand and gravel everywhere obliterated the drainage pattern which had been patiently worked out during the long period of bedrock degradation following the Appalachian Revolution. The result is the many swamps and ponds (even in the highlands) and the numerous waterfalls and twistings of the rivers as they find the sea again.

This ride begins inside the Basin at Fresh Pond, a glacial dent filled with fresh water which drains north into the Mystic River via the Alewife Brook. Meetinghouse Hill, the first of the two noticeable hills encountered on this ride, is a drumlin, characteristic of the Basin but relatively rare in the surrounding uplands. At Belmont Center, the Northern Boundary Fault makes its appearance. Pleasant St. travels along its edge, as it has since pre-Revolutionary times, when it linked Arlington Center to Waverly Sq. (which is where you had to decide whether you were going to go on to Watertown Sq. or to the center of Waltham).

Mill St. brings you into the uplands again through a nick in the edge of the fault plane made by the Beaver Brook. A fulling mill (where cloth was bleached) was established at the fault in 1662. Concord Avenue, originally called the Cambridge and Concord Turnpike, carries you over the top of Wellington Hill, across the fault, and back into the Basin to Fresh Pond again. You may be wondering why they built a road over such a steep hill when they could have gone around on the bicycle route which was already there. The Cambridge and Concord Turnpike, built during the Turnpike Era of the first couple of decades of the nineteenth century (when it was either go by horse or go on foot), was designed to connect Kendall Sq. in Cambridge

14 with the center of Concord in as straight a line as possible. The idea must have been to achieve the shortest distance at all cost between these two points, for this hard line caused the road to go over two back-breaking hills — the stage-coach changed horses in Belmont Center before attempting the first of these — and to miss Lexington Center, then a connection to the New Hampshire trade, by nearly two miles.

14 Directions

START	Entrance to FRESH POND PARK, Cambridge.
mi. 0.0	ENTER PARK and go LEFT on BIKE PATH
1.3	LEFT onto dirt path (beside smaller body of water)
1.4	LEFT onto CONCORD AVE.
2.4	LEFT onto GODEN ST.
2.5	LEFT onto SCHOOL ST.
3.7	RIGHT onto BELMONT ST.
4.0	BEAR RIGHT onto TRAPELO RD.
4.3	RIGHT onto COMMON ST. (Cushing Sq.)
5.5	LEFT onto LEONARD ST. (under bridge), then LEFT onto CONCORD AVE.
5.6	LEFT onto PLEASANT ST.
6.6	RIGHT onto TRAPELO RD.
6.8	RIGHT onto MILL ST.
7.7	RIGHT onto CONCORD AVE.
9.0	RIGHT onto LEONARD ST. (under bridge), then LEFT onto CONCORD AVE.
10.8	RIGHT onto dirt path (just before railroad tracks at second rotary), then LEFT on BIKE PATH to
11.3	START.

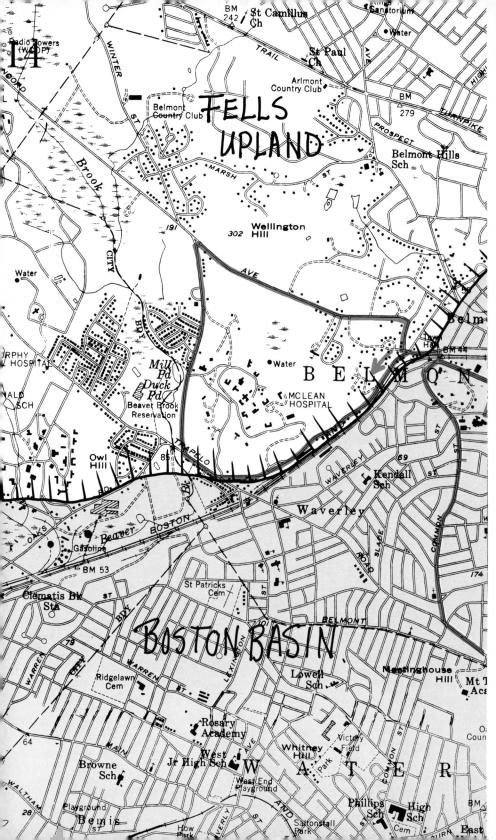

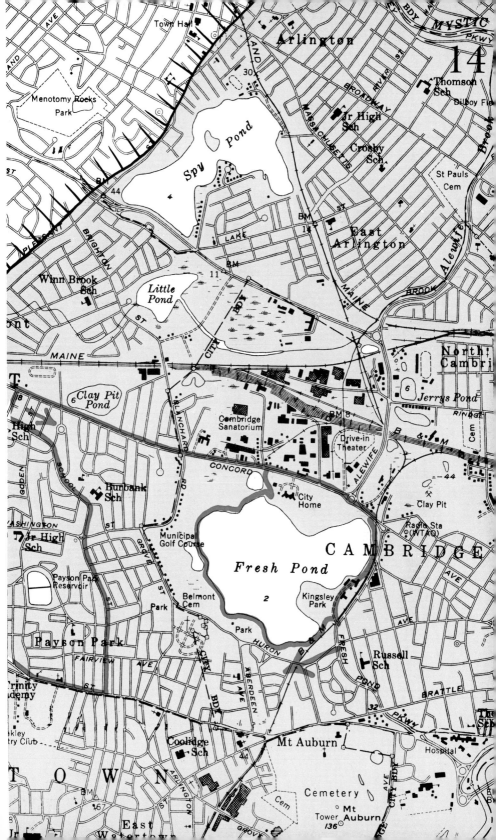

15 Lexington

This Way to the Parade Route

Few public entertainments are as popular or as simple in basic design as the parade. All that is required to ensure a reasonably good turnout and smooth procession is an occasion, people (preferably in uniform) to do the marching, refreshments, and a parade route. This last ingredient is the critical one, for a good parade route must satisfy a number of conditions at once. The streets which it follows must be wide enough to accommodate all participants, marchers and watchers alike. The road should be in good repair. And the route should go where the people tend to be. The center of town is a likely candidate.

When General Gage ordered his troops out to Concord to destroy the rebel weapons stockpiled there after the disastrous powderhouse 'bust' of 1773 in Medford, they took the parade route from East Cambridge through Arlington and Lexington. There seem to have been several considerations involved in the choice of this route. First, it was the quickest way to get from Lechmere's Point (East Cambridge) to Concord. Phase I of the plan had the British sneak out of Boston in the middle of the night from the peace and quiet of the Boston Common and go 'by sea' to nearby Lechmere's Point on the opposite shore. This was *not* a parade for the benefit of the Bostonians, who would have been sure to ride or row off in all directions toward Concord to spread the alarm, as in fact two notables, Dawes and Revere, managed to do anyway.

Second, Massachusetts Ave., then as now, afforded the gentlest terrain between Cambridge and Concord, with a large number of potential parade-watchers dwelling close by. As long as they were content to watch the parade (instead of racing off to carry a warning to Concord, as Prescott was finally able to do), the local citizens were encouraged to appreciate the display of British military might as it passed through town. (Gage had wisely ordered that soldiers be sent on ahead to watch the roads leading out of the suburban towns, a strategy decidedly less effective when applied to peninsular Boston with its practically limitless aquatic exits.)

Lexington was a high point on the march. It was a major crossroads 'out there' with several taverns, and its townfolk could be counted on to be impressed by saber-rattling, as many had participated in the French and Indian War a dozen years earlier and so knew what all those sabers were for. (In fact, many of the British-trained veterans of the French and Indian War, on their return to Lexington, had banded together with recruits from the surrounding towns to form the revolutionary Minutemen.)

The rest is history, of course: Captain Parker's welcoming committee, the exchange of shots, more a duel than a battle, and the successful rebel stand at Concord a few hours later. 'What a glorious morning for America,' as Sam Adams remarked later that day from his hiding-place in Woburn. These events are celebrated annually at Lexington and Concord with parades.

The Lexington April 19 parade customarily follows the British line of march along Massachusetts Ave. past the Monroe Tavern (commandeered by the British as a headquarters) to the Green where the Minutemen came, many from nearby Buckman Tavern, to make their stand. People come from the adjacent towns, as did their forefathers, both as spectators and participants — contemporary companies of Minutemen in eighteenth-century regalia, fife and drum corps, and reservists from Fort Devens — for Lexington is still a crossroads, as might be guessed from the numerous streets named after their destinations and radiating from Lexington Center: Lincoln St., Watertown St., Woburn St., Bedford St., and so on. (These streets customarily swap names at the border, Waltham St. in Lexington becoming Lexington St. in Waltham.)

15 Directions

START	Intersection of MILL ST. and CONCORD AVE., Belmont.
mi. 0.0	NORTHWEST on CONCORD AVE.
0.1	BEAR LEFT on CONCORD AVE.
3.2	RIGHT onto SPRING ST.
3.7	LEFT onto SHADE ST.
4.2	RIGHT onto CARY AVE.
4.6	LEFT onto MARRETT RD.
5.0	RIGHT onto LINCOLN ST.
6.0	LEFT onto WORTHEN RD., then RIGHT onto MASSACHUSETTS AVE.
6.3	BEAR RIGHT on MASSACHUSETTS AVE. (at Green)
8.4	RIGHT onto PLEASANT ST. (at rotary)
8.9	BEAR LEFT onto WATERTOWN ST. (becomes WINTER ST., Belmont)
10.3	LEFT on CONCORD AVE. to
10.4	START.

The 'British' march on Lexington Green

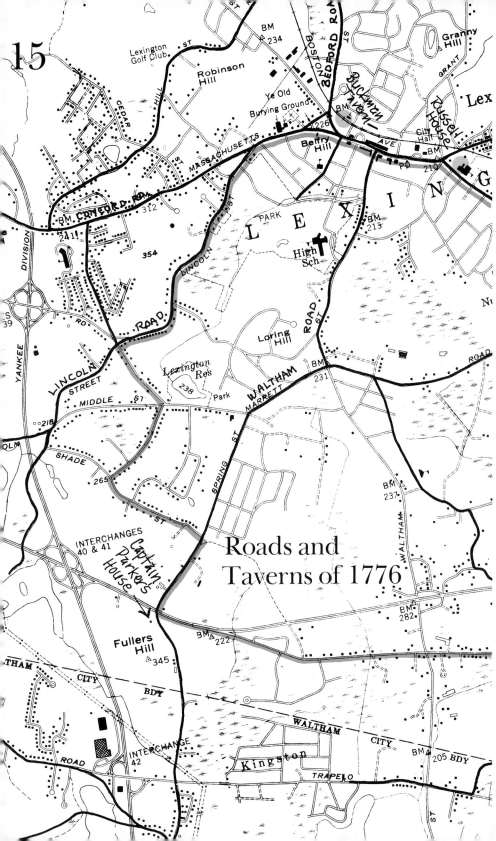

Roads and
Taverns of 1776

16   Arlington Up

Arlington is often on the way but rarely the destination. If you're going east, it's the last chance to decide whether you want to go to Cambridge (and Boston), Somerville (and Charlestown), or Medford (and the North Shore), especially if you're coming on horseback or bicycle. Similarly, if you're going northwest from Boston or Cambridge, Arlington offers the easiest route over the Northern Boundary Fault and its many attendant hills.

Unfortunately, people mostly go through without stopping, unless they happen to live here, and this has been so ever since way back when. Mill Brook is not strong enough to be an effective source of power, though some factories were hopefully built along its banks; and Arlington's other physical features, swampland and hills, have made farming improbable (if not impossible) and major crossroads few and far between.

It will come as no surprise that the only action in Arlington on April 19, 1775, took place on the way to Lexington and Concord and on the way back. Jason Russell and eleven others were captured, disarmed, and then killed at his house at Mill St., and several buildings along Massachusetts Ave. were set on fire for good measure by the British on their way through town. Subsequently, Samuel Whittemore, then eighty, killed three British soldiers before being shot, stabbed, clubbed, and left for dead. (He survived another eighteen years, as it turned out.) Earlier in the day, a contingent of old men who had not gone to Lexington decided to capture a straggling company convoy. Ensign Stephen Frost, on his way from Belmont to join his company in Lexington, met these stalwarts and had them crouch behind a roadside wall. They got the drop on the eighteen soldiers, as they demonstrated most effectively by shooting the horses dead on the first volley.

16 Directions

START	Intersection of PLEASANT ST. and MASSACHUSETTS AVE., Arlington.
mi. 0.0	SOUTHWEST on PLEASANT ST.
0.1	RIGHT onto MAPLE ST.
0.3	RIGHT onto ACADEMY ST.
0.4	LEFT onto MASSACHUSETTS AVE., then RIGHT onto MILL ST.
0.6	LEFT onto SUMMER ST.
1.1	LEFT onto BRATTLE ST.
1.3	RIGHT onto WASHINGTON ST.
1.5	LEFT onto SUMMER ST.
1.8	LEFT onto FOREST ST.
2.0	RIGHT onto FRAZER RD.
2.1	LEFT onto MILL LANE
2.2	RIGHT onto LOWELL ST.
2.4	RIGHT onto PARK AVE. EXTENSION
2.9	LEFT, then RIGHT onto FOREST ST.
3.4	LEFT onto RIDGE ST. (becomes WALTHAM ST., Woburn)
5.3	LEFT onto LEXINGTON ST. (becomes WOBURN ST., Lexington)
6.7	LEFT onto LOWELL ST.
7.0	RIGHT onto MAPLE ST.
8.0	LEFT onto MASSACHUSETTS AVE. to
11.6	START.

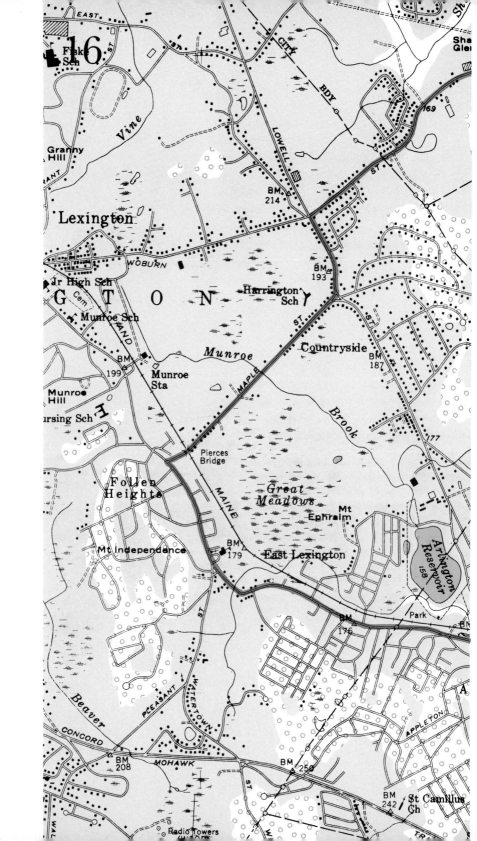

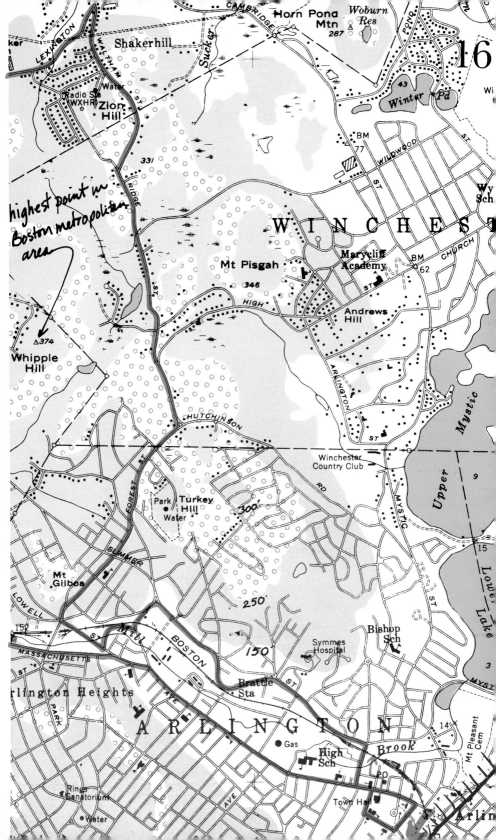

17   Down the Drain

The Arlington–Medford Waterways

Thanks to the glaciers, most of the Boston Basin is covered with piles of glacial till. The little ridge of moraine that runs from Belmont's Meetinghouse Hill all the way to mid-Cambridge, although no more than forty feet high at its highest, is still a sufficient impediment to drainage that Fresh Pond, no more than four thousand feet from the Charles River, actually drains north into the Mystic. The area around Fresh Pond — indeed much of Arlington below the Northern Boundary Fault — used to be wetlands. Fresh Pond, Little Pond, and Spy Pond were deeper basins in a vast marsh, much of which has since been filled in by man. Spy Pond drains south to the other ponds, and these are drained by the Alewife Brook which flows north into the Mystic at West Medford.

The Mystic Valley is a notch cut in the highlands above the Northern Boundary Fault. The Mystic Lakes (Upper and Lower) are fed by the Aberjona River (which drains from the northeast) and Horn Pond Brook, which carries off both the water from the back end of Mount Zion through Shaker Glen and virtually all the rainwater which falls in Woburn. The Aberjona River and Horn Pond Brook merge in Winchester.

Winchester itself represents the merger of pieces of Medford, West Cambridge (that is, Arlington), and South Woburn. The village had been named, appropriately, Waterfield since 1638 and was originally part of Charlestown. The new prosperity brought to the Mystic Valley by the building of the Middlesex Canal and the attendant industrialization of Woburn caused a marked realignment of wealth and land boundaries, and in 1850 Winchester was incorporated as an autonomous town. In a way, Winchester's relative inaccessibility, save via the Mystic Valley, made this autonomy inevitable: once the town rose to prominence, self-determination was sure to follow, given the difficulties of administering any place that can't be reached easily.

The Mystic Lakes were honored with one of the first tests of a steam-powered vessel, designed by one John Sullivan, who later successfully defended his patent rights against Robert Fulton, the man customarily given whole credit for the invention. The canal skirted the lakes on the eastern shore. It has now been filled in and the Mystic Valley Parkway constructed in its right-of-way. (Actually, farther north, the canal is still alive and well, though it's been over a century since it last saw any boat traffic.) Even where the canal has disappeared, there are still traces of its former existence: the eastern shore of the Aberjona, just before it empties into Upper Mystic Lake, will be seen to have log pilings to make its banks vertical. These are the remains of the old towpath (now entirely overgrown with secondary deciduous trees and small brush), the strategy for canal building having been to intersect existing bodies of water wherever possible at grade, shoring up one river bank for a towpath and using the river as part of the canal for as far as it led in the desired direction.

Also part of the Mystic drainage system is a series of small ponds along Rindge Avenue in Cambridge. This area has — or had — a great deal of clay which was used for bricks in the nineteenth century. The Cambridge city dump lies over the beds of some of these ponds on the theory that holes were made to be filled.

17 Directions

START	Entrance to FRESH POND PARK, Cambridge.
mi. 0.0	ENTER PARK and go LEFT on BIKE PATH
1.3	LEFT onto dirt path (beside smaller body of water)
1.4	LEFT onto CONCORD AVE.
2.0	RIGHT onto UNDERWOOD ST. (becomes HITTINGER ST.)
2.3	LEFT onto BLANCHARD ST.
3.1	RIGHT onto PLEASANT ST.
4.2	STRAIGHT (across Massachusetts Ave.) onto MYSTIC ST. (= Rte. 3)
6.1	RIGHT onto EVERETT ST.
6.5	RIGHT onto BACON ST.
6.6	RIGHT onto MYSTIC VALLEY PARKWAY
8.7	BEAR LEFT onto LINCOLN ST.
9.1	RIGHT onto HARVARD AVE. (and cross Mystic Valley Parkway)
9.3	LEFT onto DECATUR ST.
9.6	RIGHT onto MYSTIC VALLEY PARKWAY
9.7	RIGHT onto ROUTE 16
10.7	LEFT onto MASSACHUSETTS AVE.
11.1	RIGHT onto CEDAR ST. (at railroad tracks)
11.4	RIGHT onto RINDGE AVE.
11.5	LEFT onto SHERMAN ST.
12.0	RIGHT onto WALDEN ST.
12.4	RIGHT onto HURON AVE.
12.8	CROSS FRESH POND PARKWAY to SIDEWALK, then RIGHT along SIDEWALK to
13.0	START.

18 On the Canal

Winchester–Woburn

Loammi Baldwin and a small group of his friends from Medford thought it would be a fine thing to build a canal to connect the Merrimack River with the tidal waters of the Mystic, that is, Medford, preferably taking in Woburn on the way. The Merrimack, running from central New Hampshire southeast to the Atlantic, was a carrier of substantial trade which might as well have been diverted to Medford via canal as allowed to continue along its established course to Newburyport.

On consideration of the amount of capital that would be necessary to finance the construction of such a canal, Baldwin and friends had an even better idea: why not get some wealthy Boston businessmen to help pay the tab and have the canal go through to Boston? The traffic could still stop in Medford (and Woburn) and in any event the value of the land near the canal would be bound to go up, as generally happens with the land next to a major transportation line. This, naturally, was a serious consideration for people whose holdings were primarily in land.

The appropriate Bostonians were found and in 1793 a charter was granted the now slightly expanded group. Then began the real financial troubles. First, of course, the canal cost a great deal more to build than had been anticipated. Original cost estimates had been unrealistic, largely because no canals had ever been built here before — the Middlesex Canal was one of the first two to be built in North America — and so nobody really knew what was involved. It was not long before the Medford contingent was forced out, leaving the Bostonians, with their superior financial resources, in control.

Not that the Bostonians then made a killing on the canal traffic. Indeed, once the canal was finally completed (in 1803), it led a relatively short and impoverished life. It had long been hoped that the canal would be able to compete favorably with the teamsters who, with their teams of horses, had been hauling freight inland and out ever since a producing and consuming inland had been established. What happened was a price war which the canal proved unable to win. The deathblow was dealt by the railroad, the newest, quickest mode of transportation and, next to the horse team, the most far-ranging. The canal was quite defunct by 1850.

For the original canal-backers, many of whose sons were instrumental in bringing the railroads to the region, it had by no means been a total loss. The land values along the canal (and later the railroad) did in fact go up as anticipated as new industries settled in the area. The Bostonians, who had all along been less interested in the immediate rewards of shipping, toll-collecting, and water power rental than in the many long-term gains to be had from the opening up of the hinterlands, also had little cause for complaint.

And as for wise old Loammi Baldwin, he didn't do too badly either. Having never bought stock in the canal, preferring instead to draw a salary from the company for his services, he spent his spare time developing the Baldwin apple while his sons set themselves up as some of the country's first civil engineers.

18 Directions

START	Intersection of MT. VERNON ST. and MAIN ST., Winchester.
mi. 0.0	EAST on MT. VERNON ST.
0.2	LEFT onto WASHINGTON ST.
4.1	LEFT onto MISHAWUM RD.
4.9	STRAIGHT onto SCHOOL ST.
5.9	LEFT onto MERRIMAC ST.
6.0	LEFT onto MAIN ST., then RIGHT onto ELM ST.
6.7	LEFT, then RIGHT onto ROUTE 38 SOUTH (= MAIN ST.)
8.4	STRAIGHT onto PLEASANT ST.
8.7	LEFT onto ARLINGTON RD.
9.5	BEAR RIGHT onto POND ST.
9.9	LEFT onto WOODSIDE RD.
10.5	STRAIGHT onto WILDWOOD ST.
10.7	RIGHT onto FLETCHER ST.
11.0	CROSS CHURCH ST. onto BACON ST.
11.6	LEFT onto MYSTIC VALLEY PARKWAY
12.2	LEFT onto MAIN ST. to
12.3	START.

Shawsheen Aqueduct, the Middlesex Canal

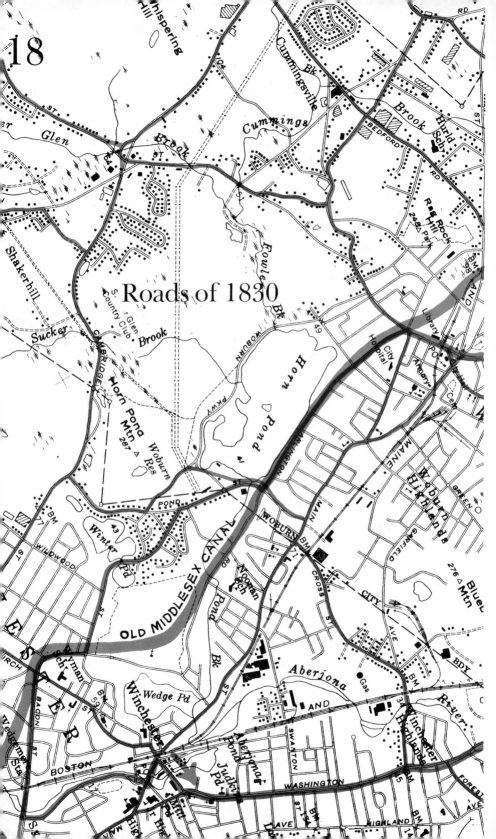

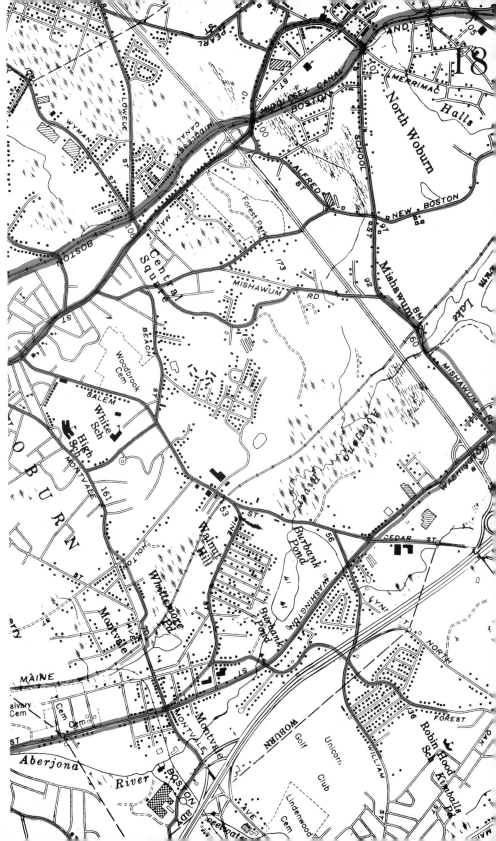

19 A Zoo and a View (Or Two)

Medford–Stoneham

As you turn up Governors Ave. in Medford, you will see outcroppings of the great Medford dike, first on your left, then on your right, as you cross it. A dike is formed when molten rock forces its way up through a crack in the earth's crust. Since the Medford dike crosses the Northern Boundary Fault intact, it must have been formed after the fault.

No one knows how large or how deep the dike is because, like a giant sea serpent emerging periodically above the waves, only the highest portions of the dike are visible. The rest has not yet been exposed by the erosion of the rocks around it. Even so, outcroppings can be seen for almost three miles in a line from Powderhouse Sq. to just south of Spot Pond. The tapering end of the dike in Powderhouse Sq. is jammed with pieces from the walls of the crack which were carried or torn loose by the lava as it pushed upward. In places where the rock has been exposed for a long time, the characteristic lobed or spheroidal weathering pattern can be seen. Where the Fellsway crosses the northern end of the dike, a dramatic cross-section has been created by recent expressway construction. The Pine Hill lookout tower (reached by path from South Border Rd.) accents the highest point of the dike.

The section of the ride on paths through the Fells Reservation gets off to a great start by going down a soapbox derby racetrack. The pace changes abruptly, though, at the end of the track and is necessarily slow and cautious for the next (unpaved) half mile or so. As you come around the bend among boulders of the metamorphic Marlboro formation, you will see some of the oldest rocks in the area (dating back more than 600 million years). Irregular terrain like this provides lookout posts and hiding-places for small mammals as well as a wide variety of drainage, soil, and temperature conditions supporting a healthy diversity of plants. Much can be read from small clues in the landscape and the details of its 'furniture.' A small footprint at the edge of a drying mud puddle tells of a raccoon's visit, while a soft wad of gray fur and tiny bones under a large tree tells of the portion of an owl's dinner that wasn't digested. Spit up after dinner while the owl rests high in the tree, these 'pellets' contain the smallest sculptures in the museum-without-walls.

Parts of the road from here can be ridden even on a delicate ten-speed racer, but some rough sections should be walked. This interlude provides a woodland experience normally available to hikers only, winding up at Bear Hill (formerly, Bare Hill) Lookout Tower. Though profusely littered with broken glass, a climb to the top affords a view all the way to New Hampshire. An unusually clear set of scratches made by the passing glacier some years ago is visible on the surface of the bedrock along the path leading down to North Border Rd. from the lookout tower. From there, the road is paved again through quaint old Stoneham and along the shore of Spot Pond. A list of recent zoo births is posted at the front entrance. In keeping with its function of housing captive animals is the inclusion in the zoo compound of a kennel for police dogs and a stable for the MDC mounted police horses.

The last section of this ride through Wright Park (from the bottom of Spot Pond to the Fellsway) is the last chance to enjoy a peaceful moment or two before joining the traffic headed back to Medford Sq.

19 Directions

START   MEDFORD SQUARE, Medford.

mi. 0.0   NORTHWEST on HIGH ST.

0.1   RIGHT onto GOVERNORS AVE.

1.0   RIGHT onto SOUTH BORDER RD. (at end of Governors Ave.)

1.2   BEAR RIGHT on SOUTH BORDER RD. (at fork)

1.3   LEFT (around Roosevelt Circle) onto FELLSWAY WEST (= Rte. 28 North)

2.9   LEFT into FELLS RESERVATION (first road after turn-off for parking lot), then
RIGHT onto PATH, then
LEFT (up hill) on PAVED PATH

3.1   RIGHT onto SOAPBOX DERBY RACE-TRACK

3.4   RIGHT (at end of track)

3.5   LEFT (uphill at intersection of paths near old railroad bridge)

4.1   RETRACE (from LOOKOUT TOWER) to first
RIGHT (down hill), then

4.2   RIGHT (just past concrete slab), then next
RIGHT onto NORTH BORDER RD. (industrial park on left)

4.6   RIGHT on NORTH BORDER RD. (under Rte. 93)

4.7   LEFT onto PARK ST.

4.9   RIGHT onto MARBLE ST.

5.2   LEFT onto MAIN ST. (= Rte. 28)

5.6   BEAR RIGHT onto CENTRAL ST.

5.7   RIGHT onto COMMON ST.

5.8   RIGHT onto PINE ST. (at end of common)

6.0   LEFT onto FRANKLIN ST.

6.1   RIGHT onto POND ST.

7.0   BEAR LEFT on POND ST. (at reservoir)

7.3   RIGHT (into Zoo parking lot), then
RIGHT onto POND ST.

7.7   BEAR RIGHT onto WOODLAND RD.

8.4   RIGHT onto MDC PATH

8.8   BEAR LEFT (just past water pipe depository)

8.9   LEFT (at fork below huge boulders)
9.1   LEFT onto FELLSWAY
10.3   BEAR RIGHT onto FOREST ST. (at Roosevelt
       Circle) to
11.1   START.

Junior, the pygmy hippopotamus in the Stoneham Zoo

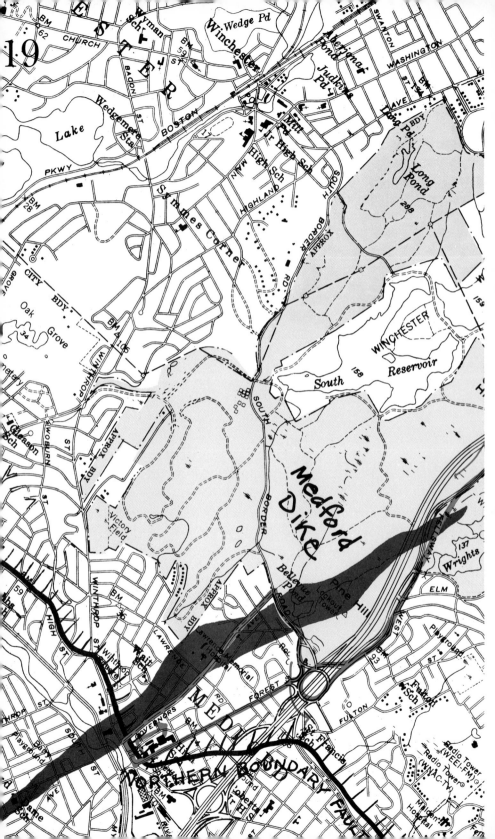

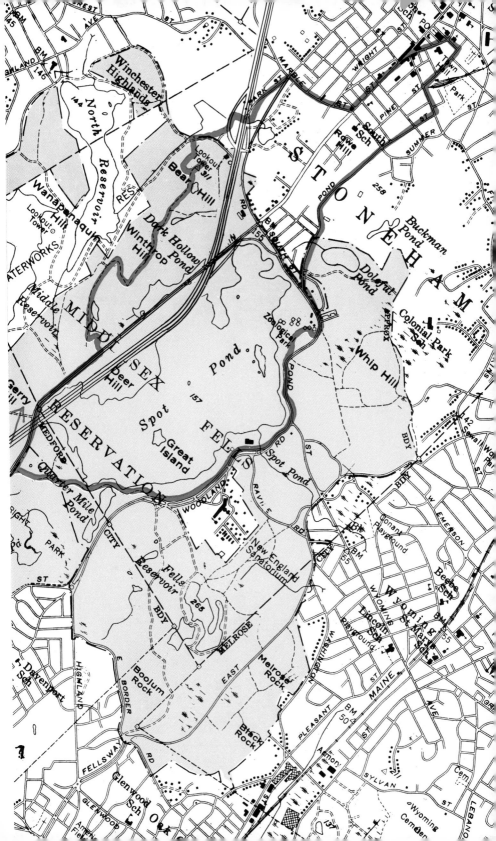

Section 4

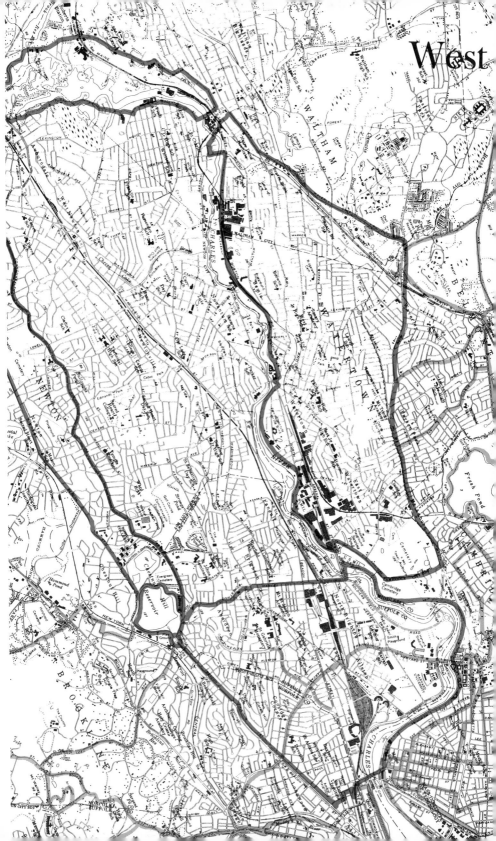

20 Home Delivery

Newton

It is said that Mohammed went to the mountain because the mountain had previously let it be known that it would be unable (or unwilling) to come to Mohammed. This is a familiar scenario: if you want something *there* which can't (or won't) come *here,* you have to go from here to there to get it. Roads were invented to facilitate overland passage from here to there and back.

Mohammed could, of course, have stayed here at home and had the mountain brought to him. This would have involved a series of complicated arrangements with his broker, his banker, and a company specializing in land removal. To facilitate such complicated arrangements, paper was invented.

With the invention of both roads and paper, another scenario suggests itself: Mohammed could simply have written the mountain a letter and sent it by courier. Aware of these various possibilities, England discouraged any substantial road-building in the Colonies. As long as communication among the colonial towns was hampered by the lack of good roads, England could stay in charge *here* at the hub, and the towns could remain *there* at the far end of their individual spokes.

Here and *there* are relative, of course, and it is usually only a matter of time before the people living *there* begin to think of it as *here,* and of the old *here* as *there.* The first post road was built between New York and Boston in the early 1670's. Scarcely a century later, England had to sign for the Declaration of Independence (return receipt having been requested). Shortly thereafter, Ben Franklin became our first Postmaster General.

Some of the earliest paper to travel over the post road was undoubtedly newspaper. Some newspapers are still delivered by post, though, with the proliferation of morning, evening, and Sunday editions and an expanding suburban readership, most newspaper companies have set up their own streamlined distribution systems.

This ride travels the length of residential Newton, a town in which a staggering amount of newspaper is delivered every day. There are local newspapers — some sections of Newton read the Waltham paper, others the Newton paper — and several Boston dailies (morning, evening, and Sunday), as well as the ubiquitous *New York Times*. Many people subscribe to two or three of these papers, to keep in touch with what is going on in several 'heres': right here, here in the Boston area, here in the East, and so on.

Papers are delivered in Newton in the following way. Each newspaper company has at least one outlet in Newton. This is usually owned by the newspaper company, though other arrangements are possible. The *New York Times,* for example, is delivered in the area covered by this ride through an outlet owned by one of the larger Boston papers. Each outlet is supplied with so many newspapers per day for local delivery. The papers are then carried from the outlet to homes and local newsstands by a small army of paper-boys, paper-girls, their younger siblings, and teams of driver-deliverers, each along his or her paper route.

The general outlines of each individual route are set by the outlet, which considers population density, how safe the roads are for cyclists (and their younger siblings), how many papers can be carried by the deliverer, and who's likely to be available to do the delivering. The individual paper-deliverer is then given a list of subscribers and is free to put together the best itinerary he or she can, generally though not necessarily a minor variation on the route worked out by the previous entrepreneur.

20   Directions

START   CLEVELAND CIRCLE, Brighton.
mi. 0.0   NORTHWEST on CHESTNUT HILL AVE.
0.2   LEFT onto COMMONWEALTH AVE.
1.9   BEAR RIGHT onto one-way lane of COMMONWEALTH AVE.
5.2   LEFT onto WASHINGTON ST. (= Rte. 16)
6.1   LEFT onto BEACON ST. to
11.8   START.

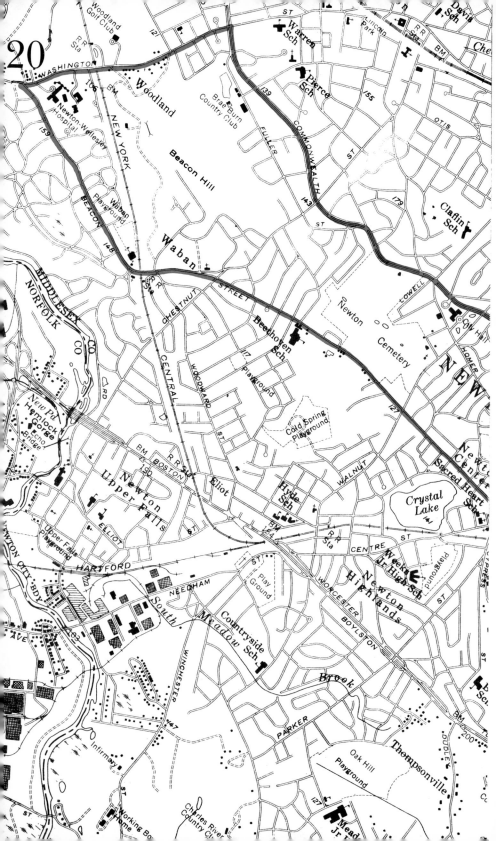

21 The Brighton Cake Walk

One Wedge

Why did the cyclist climb the hill? The Classics suggest two possible explanations for this seemingly irrational behavior: (1) 'to get to the other side,' and (2) 'to see what he could see.' A combination of these two is also possible, as is suggested by this ride, which offers a plain and easy introduction to The Hill'in practically all its glory.

Hills are formed in a variety of ways. Igneous activity can send molten rock up from inside the earth to make domes and dikes; glaciers can bulldoze (or carry in their pockets) the materials for moraines, eskers, and drumlins; rivers can cut valleys; and the earth's crust itself can buckle, tilt, and fold when really provoked.

The elements (and man) conspire to alter the original shape of hills. Wind and water take their toll, generally concentrating their erosive activities on a particular side of the hill, since weather tends to travel only a few tried and true routes. If left to their own devices, wind and water together would eventually smooth away all the earth's wrinkles, but they are kept from so doing by the periodic occurrence (or recurrence) of one or another of the hill-making processes just mentioned. (Boston has witnessed several major glaciations so far.)

So hills come in different shapes and sizes. More to the point, hill *sides* come in a variety of shapes and sizes, some having gentler slopes and some getting a better class of weather, two important factors to consider if you're planning to build a road or a house (or both).

The Boston Basin is a little like a wedge of layer cake that has first been sat on and then generously iced with a rather lumpy frosting. This ride starts from the depressed end, follows a gradually ascending furrow in the frosting (Beacon St.) in the general direction of the (relatively) un-sat-upon end, then abruptly descends over the side (Chestnut Hill Ave.–Market St.) to the plate (the Charles River).

Beacon St. is a groove in the frosting on several grounds: it passes by a number of glacial lumps (Aspinwall Hill, Corey Hill, Fisher Hill) typical of the top layer of the cake, and it has a certain homogeneity of population as well. (Beacon St. is about as uniformly white-collar as you can get for the money.)

Chestnut Hill Ave.–Market St., by contrast, is a cross-section, though Boston University's demographic till and the generally rising cost of living are beginning to shake up residence patterns in such a way as to obscure the original strata. There are still discernible bands of well-to-do Jews, less well-to-do Jews, well-to-do Catholics, less well-to-do Catholics (each of the latter clustering in different ethnic and linguistic substrata), and the not nearly so well-to-do, whose neighborhoods are, as is the usual practice, bounded by high-speed roads, railroad tracks, and water.

21 Directions

START   Intersection of BU BRIDGE and COMMONWEALTH AVE., Boston.

mi. 0.0   SOUTHEAST on ESSEX ST., then

        BEAR LEFT (at gas station) on MOUNTFORT ST., then

        HAIRPIN RIGHT onto LENOX ST., then immediately

        LEFT onto PRESCOTT ST.

        LEFT onto IVY ST.

        RIGHT onto CHILTON ST.

        LEFT onto CHURCHILL ST.

        RIGHT onto CARLTON ST.

0.5   RIGHT onto BEACON ST.

2.7   CROSS, CHESTNUT HILL AVE. on BEACON ST. (at Cleveland Circle)

3.7   BEAR RIGHT onto CHESTNUT HILL DRIVEWAY (between reservoir and Boston College)

3.9   BEAR RIGHT on CHESTNUT HILL DRIVEWAY (at fork)

4.4   RIGHT onto COMMONWEALTH AVE.

4.5   SHARP LEFT onto CHESTNUT HILL AVE. (at lights) (becomes MARKET ST. at Brighton Center)

6.2   LEFT onto ARSENAL ST.

6.3   RIGHT onto CHARLES GOODENOUGH BLVD. (just across river)

7.4   JOIN MDC BIKE PATH (on right at boathouse)

9.7   RIGHT over BU BRIDGE to

9.9   START.

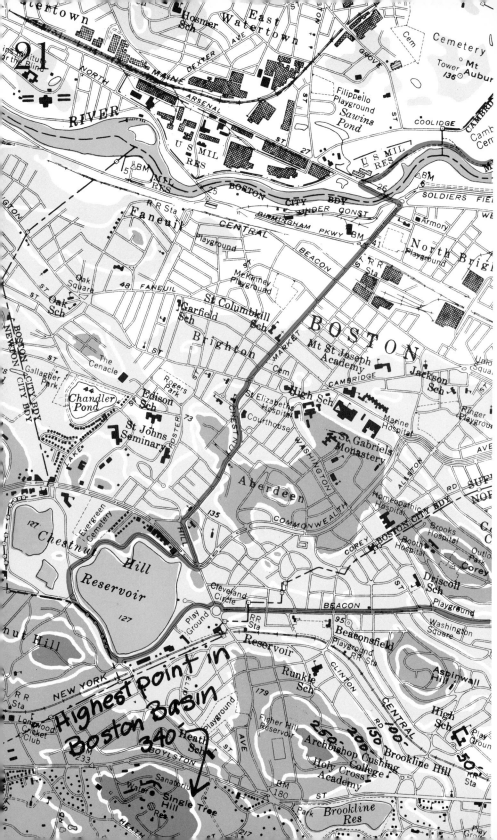

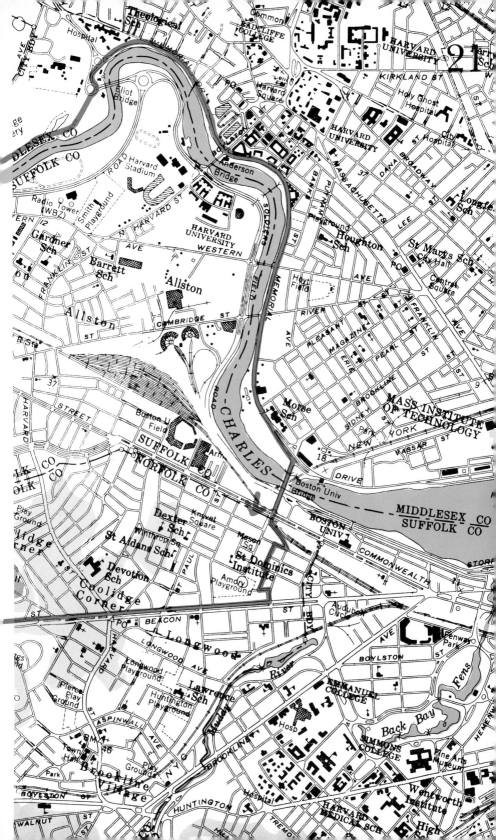

22 Watertown Bound

When Governor Winthrop sailed into Boston Harbor on June 17, 1630, he was looking for a place where about seven hundred people could plant in one big harmonious settlement. He was already in trouble and things were about to get worse. His plans to move in (harmoniously) with the people already settled in Salem had proved unworkable in the five days since he had arrived from England. Now, heading up the Charles, he had to decide between STRAIGHT on CHARLES R. and RIGHT onto MYSTIC R. By early July, everyone had temporarily set up in Charlestown (where the two rivers come together) while the debate about which way to go continued between Winthrop and Deputy Governor Dudley. Before they could decide on any one place for all, disease, overcrowding, and the threat of marauding French forced Winthrop to accept dispersed settlement. Sir Richard Saltonstall, a large investor in the Massachusetts Bay Company, was the first to depart, establishing his group in Watertown by the end of July.

As Governor of the Mass. Bay Co., Winthrop was essentially the chairman of the board of a large corporation. Saltonstall was one of the backers who had used his influence to get permission from the British government for corporate H.Q. to be set up in Newe rather than Olde England. A good businessman out to protect his investment, he knew how useful it would be to be able to make on-the-spot decisions, such as where to plant the first inland settlement in Mass. Bay.

Dispersed settlements were not part of Winthrop's original, apparently rather vague plans and no provision had been made for them in the company charter brought over from

England. When Saltonstall and his group left for Watertown, organizational decisions were made whose effects laid the ground rules for the politics of land use ever since. By opting for Congregationalism, in which the covenant of a church's first communicants provided the legal basis for local government, the chairman of the board and his assistants set the evolution of the New England township in motion. Company control was maintained by granting land only to groups of people who, by forming a church, indicated their willingness to be governed.

The combination of Congregational Puritanism with corporate control over land titles quickly produced boundary lines all over the Massachusetts map. A modern map of Watertown shows some of the ways in which this happened. The settlements of 1630 were not recognized as towns for six years, and it was another two years before they began to encroach upon each other, necessitating the (fairly) careful laying-out of the original boundaries. When this was done, Waltham and Weston, along with chunks of Cambridge, Belmont, Lincoln, and Concord, were still part of Watertown.

Nucleated settlement, which had eluded Winthrop, was now enforced at the local level. Everybody was supposed to live within half a mile of the church, with the surrounding lands parceled out in proportion to individual investment in the town. As local resources became scarce with the growth of towns, subgroups, whose political discontent could find expression in the theology of the minister they chose, would reestablish themselves elsewhere as if they were one of the many new groups arriving from England. Watertown helped fill up the Connecticut River Valley in this way during the 1630's.

When the map filled up, towns began to subdivide without migration. The farmers of peripheral town land frequently had seasonal dwellings on their farms to cut down on commuting time from their homes near the church. When several farmhouses were in the same area, the residents of these villages would sometimes hire their own minister, thereby avoiding town on Sundays as well as the other days of the week. Having to pay for both their own and the town's ministers was a frequent source of discontent.

22

Before finally being set off as Weston in 1712, Watertown Farms battled over this issue for twenty-five years. (Malden's earlier separation from Charlestown had come as the result of similar battles.) The setting off of Waltham (like Weston, on the far side of town from Boston) in 1738 over the question of where to put the schoolhouse (for which everyone chipped in) is another example of the way in which the division of interests of townsmen led to the division of their towns.

22 Directions

START	Intersection of MT. AUBURN ST. and COOLIDGE AVE., Cambridge.
mi. 0.0	WEST on MT. AUBURN ST.
0.6	RIGHT onto BELMONT ST.
1.7	BEAR RIGHT onto TRAPELO RD.
3.3	STRAIGHT on TRAPELO RD. (in left-hand lane, just after Waverly Sq.)
3.5	LEFT onto WAVERLY OAKS RD. (at lights)
5.2	STRAIGHT onto LINDEN ST.
5.3	RIGHT onto MAIN ST.
5.8	LEFT onto ELM ST.
6.3	LEFT onto BENEFIT ST.
6.4	LEFT onto NEWTON ST.
6.6	RIGHT onto RIVER ST. (becomes PLEASANT ST., Watertown)
9.1	RIGHT into WATERTOWN SQ., then immediately BEAR LEFT past ROUTE 16 WEST, then immediately
9.2	RIGHT onto MDC BIKE PATH (next to river)
10.3	RIGHT onto RIVER ST. (end of bike path), then
10.4	RIGHT onto NORTH BEACON ST.
10.6	LEFT onto CHARLES RIVER RD. (just before bridge), then REJOIN BIKE PATH
11.3	LEFT onto ARSENAL ST.
11.4	RIGHT onto COOLIDGE AVE. to
12.7	START.

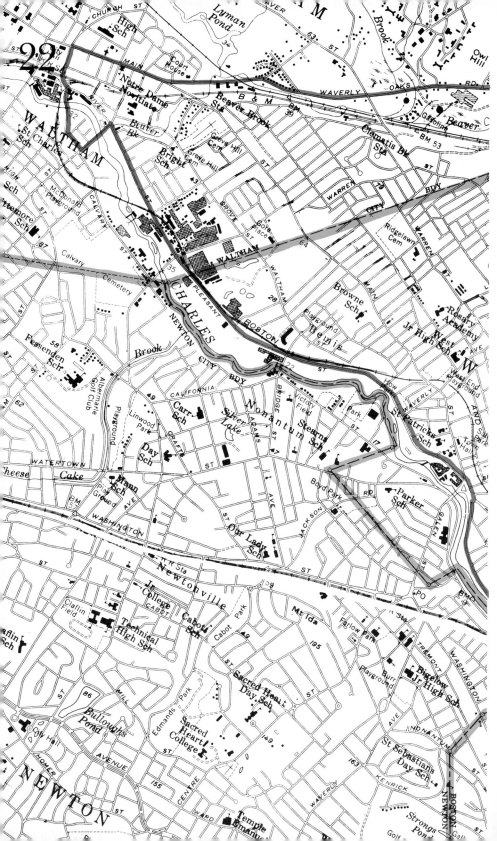

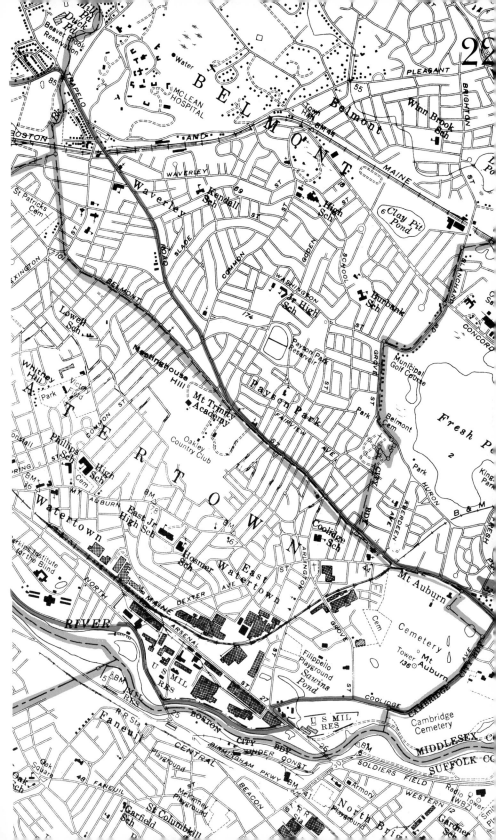

23 The American System

Waltham–Newton Lower Falls

Winding its way through the erratic glacial topography of the Boston Basin, the Charles River has been and continues to be used in a wide variety of ways. One of these, characteristic of New England in the last century, was for water power to run mills. This route takes in both sides of the river from Newton Lower Falls to the falls at 'Eden Vale' in Waltham, showing contrasting land uses which give some idea of how much a sudden ten-foot drop of the river (as at Waltham) can mean for an area. Because of its cheap power and proximity to Boston, Waltham became an important site for the social and technological experiments of a few wealthy Bostonians striving to introduce Americans to the factory in the early 1800's.

The imperial face-off between England and France gave Boston merchants the chance to pick up some extra capital by operating out of their 'neutral port.' When England threatened to sink anyone trading with France and France offered to sink everyone else, those same merchants found themselves casting about for something else to invest in. With his textile import business hampered by the British after 1812, Francis Cabot Lowell joined with some of his brothers-in-law to see what heavy investment could do for domestic production.

Industrial spying was a well-established tradition long before Lowell returned from England in 1812 with a good idea of how to make the newly developed power loom and an equally vivid image of the social problems he was likely to face in getting people to work in a factory. In fact, the Massachusetts legislature had helped finance an expedition to England to get prohibited models of spinning jennies in

1786. One of New England's many mills which developed by imitating British technology had already been in Waltham for several years when Lowell's group spent $1,000 on water rights there. But Lowell's newly formed Boston Manufacturing Co. used its vast resources ($400,000) to put together an unbeatable combination of technology and labor control.

Until Lowell's company put weaving into the same factory with spinning, high labor costs had kept down investment in textile manufacture. Weavers working under the old putting-out system just couldn't be controlled like unmarried women living in strictly supervised company dormitories. The company's interest in its employees' morals encouraged rural parents to send their daughters to the factory where it was quickly learned that 'morality' usually meant long hours (eighty a week) at tedious jobs. Having found a way to get people to work harder than they ever would at home, the company expanded so rapidly that local competition was bought out by 1819, and by 1823 Lowell moved to the Merrimack River for more water power. With the bugs worked out of the system in Waltham, newly named Lowell was set up as the world's first complete company town, complete even to having European agents recruiting the immigrants who began to swell the population of American cities.

An investment in textiles was also an investment in the slave-based production of the South, as the complexity of Boston's abolition politics showed later on. But while the Civil War was the beginning of the end for textiles in the North, it also gave a much-needed boost to another of Waltham's industrial experiments. The problem of developing machinery for a textile mill was nothing compared to what the Waltham Watch Co. went through to develop mass-produced watches. The need for small-scale precision to make interchangeable parts was the technological stumbling block to be overcome by the 'American System' of watchmaking. Even though interchangeable parts also means interchangeable machinists, the plan to lower the price of a watch by reducing labor costs was not an overnight success. In fact, new cheap watches didn't sell fast enough to pay for the expensive research and development needed to get the business going. The company which had

23 come to Waltham for its clean air in 1854 was bankrupt by 1857. People just weren't that interested in knowing the correct time even if it could be had more cheaply than ever before.

But the Civil War changed all that. The demand for cheap soldiers' watches paid back the investors who had bought out the company a few years earlier, and the thoroughly industrialized postwar society was so time-conscious that Waltham became 'Watch City.'

23 Directions

START	Intersection of CONCORD ST. and WASHINGTON ST. (= Rte. 16), Newton Lower Falls.
mi. 0.0	NORTH on CONCORD ST.
1.5	RIGHT onto SOUTH AVE. (= Rte. 30)
1.9	LEFT onto RIVER RD. (entrances to Mass. Turnpike), then
2.0	RIGHT onto NORUMBEGA RD.
2.9	RIGHT onto SOUTH ST. (first right)
4.4	RIGHT onto HIGHLAND ST. (towards hospital)
4.6	LEFT onto PROSPECT ST., then next
4.7	RIGHT onto CHARLES ST.
5.3	RIGHT onto MOODY ST. (end of Charles St.)
5.5	RIGHT onto CRESCENT ST.
6.3	RIGHT onto WOERD AVE.
6.9	STRAIGHT onto FOREST GROVE RD. (dirt, at far side of paved loop)
7.7	EXIT park LEFT onto ISLINGTON ST., then immediately RIGHT onto COMMONWEALTH AVE.
7.9	HAIRPIN LEFT onto WOODBINE ST.
8.1	RIGHT onto AUBURN ST.
8.2	LEFT onto WOODLAND RD. (over Lasell Bridge)
8.3	RIGHT onto HANCOCK ST.
8.5	STRAIGHT onto GROVE ST.
9.6	RIGHT onto HAGAR PATH (at one way sign), then
9.7	LEFT onto CONCORD ST. to
9.8	START.

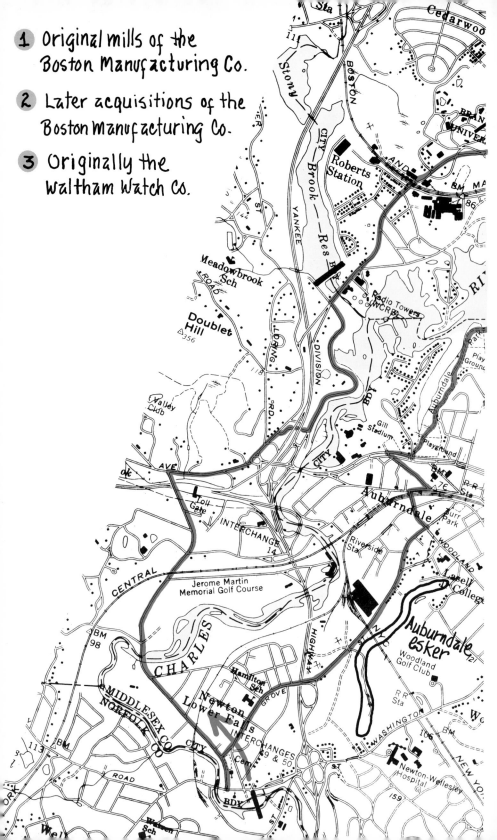

1 Original mills of the Boston Manufacturing Co.

2 Later acquisitions of the Boston Manufacturing Co.

3 Originally the Waltham Watch Co.

24　Away

Newton Lower Falls–Newton Upper Falls

Where people go when they pick themselves up and move some place else is Away. Where people go when they daydream is also Away. The only difference is that the daydreamer doesn't have to go to the bother of moving.

While this mode of travel has a number of obvious points in its favor, there is a hitch: society discourages daydreaming, especially in the presence of other people who might take the daydreamer's characteristic inattention to all and everyone around him personally. Fortunately, society would seem to have a strong daydreamer lobby which has managed to have had set aside a number of public places in which daydreaming will be tolerated.

Beaches, for example, are acceptable places to daydream, though this is often easier said than done, as beaches are also acceptable places to run around and make a lot of noise. Woods with trails in them, such as are found all over Lincoln and Concord, are likely prospects too, though daydreamers are generally expected to do their daydreaming on foot. (One of the rules about being Away seems to be that you have to look as though you were doing something other than just daydreaming: 'hiking,' 'getting a tan,' or the like.)

Not every place has a beach or woodland trails, of course. Cities generally have neither. Urban daydreamers have a number of places they can go for some relatively undisturbed daydreaming. There are parks, of course, many of which come equipped with benches which have been thoughtfully provided by the local department of parks or by the MDC. Benches suitable for daydreaming may also be found outside such public buildings as the library and city hall. The steps of at least *some* public buildings, such as the post office in Central Sq., Cambridge, count as benches.

The Newton Lower Falls–Newton Upper Falls ride contains examples of two further possibilities. Both of these, as is appropriate for the sort of town in which they occur, assume that the daydreamer has a car, though this is by no means a must. One Away place is the paved road which peters out into a dirt road at the edge of the woods. These come in two kinds: 'dead-end' and 'through.' (In the first, the road simply ends; in the second, the pavement resumes at the other side of the woods.) An example of the 'through' road is offered by 4th Ave. on this ride.

A higher-class, though consequently more popular Away place is typified by Quinobequin Road: the MDC parkway. As the name implies, parkways attempt to combine the best features of the park and the road. They therefore tend to be green with trees, often follow a river, and are generally quiet enough in off hours to allow daydreamers to park along them. Like roads, they are supposed to take you somewhere, but as all cyclists know, you don't have to be stationary to be Away.

24 Directions

START   Intersection of RIVER ST. and WASHING-
TON ST. (= Rte. 16), Wellesley.

mi. 0.0	SOUTHEAST on RIVER ST.
0.3	CROSS WALNUT ST. onto CEDAR ST.
1.3	BEAR LEFT on CEDAR ST.
1.9	LEFT onto CENTRAL AVE., then next
2.0	RIGHT onto WEBSTER ST.
2.7	LEFT onto GREENDALE AVE.
3.0	LEFT on GREENDALE AVE.
3.4	LEFT onto KENDRICK ST.
4.0	LEFT onto 4th AVE.
4.4	STRAIGHT (disregard DEAD END sign)
4.8	STRAIGHT (pavement ends)
4.9	RIGHT onto NEEDHAM ST.
5.0	LEFT onto OAK ST.
5.3	LEFT onto CHESTNUT ST.
5.8	LEFT onto ELLIS ST.
6.0	CROSS BOYLSTON ST. (= Rte. 9) onto QUINOBEQUIN RD.
7.9	LEFT onto ROUTE 16, then immediately LEFT onto WALES ST. (becomes WALNUT ST., Wellesley)
8.2	RIGHT onto RIVER ST. to
8.5	START.

Newton Lower Falls

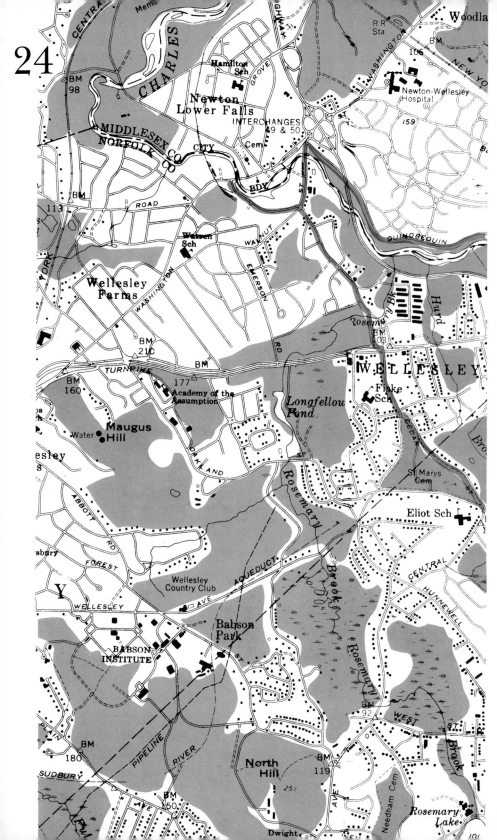

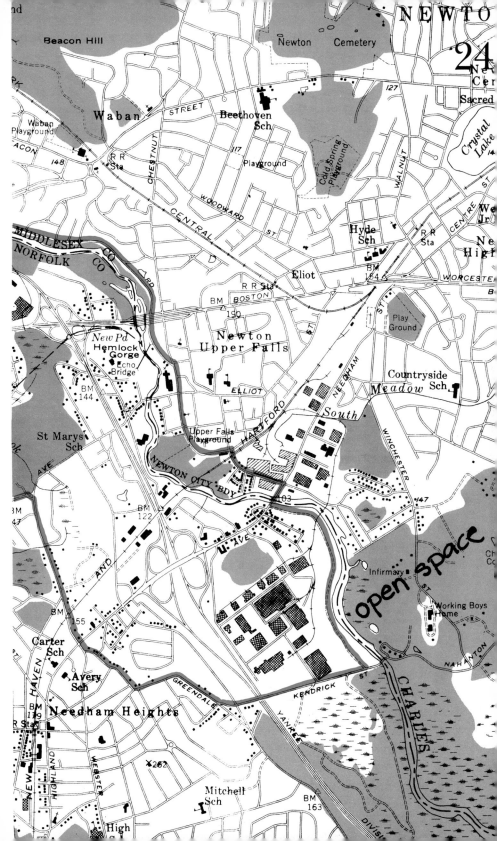

25 Contentment-on-the-Charles

Dedham

When they petitioned the General Court in 1636 to be set up as an autonomous plantation, the citizens of Dedham asked that their town be named 'Contentment.' For some reason, somebody in the legislature proposed that the town be named 'Dedham' instead, and so it was. All things considered, 'Contentment' was probably an apt choice, for Dedham has remained prosperous, quiet, and content virtually from the start.

Greendale Ave. (Needham) is on the high side of the Mother Brook Fault, the major boundary fault to the west which, with the Northern and Southern Boundary Faults, provides a geological definition for the Boston Basin. Long after the uplands were free of ice, the last vestiges of the great glacier clung to the lowlands of the Basin. This forced the rivers which drained the western uplands to find outlets around the Blue Hills to the south or through the valley of the Merrimack to the north. When the ice finally disappeared altogether, the rivers feeding into the Basin were obliged to weave new channels among the great piles of gravel and debris which had been left all over the place. Hence the Charles River bangs a sharp left on entering the Basin, and meanders back and forth along the Mother Brook Fault all the way up to Waltham, where the river is deflected east by the still protruding cliffs of the Northern Boundary Fault. The more modest elevation which occasionally marks the location of the Mother Brook Fault is best appreciated at the crossing of Route 128 on Kendrick St., just south of Newton Upper Falls. As an added bonus, the last five hundred feet or so of Greendale Ave. before the turn onto Kendrick St. are laid out along the spine of an esker, a bed of sediment left by a melt-water stream traveling under the ice (or along a crack) of a glacier.

The Charles River's local entrance to the Basin proved a boon in two respects. Incoming water could be used to power mills. (The connection of the Charles River to the Mother Brook — formerly East Brook, later Mill Brook — was undertaken with this use of the water in mind scarcely three years after the settlers had unpacked and made themselves at home.) It also served to isolate the town to an extent, thereby allowing its citizens to go about their business, which was generally brisk.

Actually, Dedham wasn't as isolated as all that, for a number of fairly important roads pass through town. First, there was the Boston–Providence post road, then, in the early 1800's, the Norfolk and Bristol Turnpike and the Hartford and Dedham Turnpike. The Norfolk and Bristol Turnpike ran from Dedham Court House to Providence. It was brought into being, amid much grumbling on the part of some Dedham residents ('Many dread it as bad as a standing Army to sponge them of money'), to replace the shoddy post road. It runs north to Boston on Washington St.

Still, Dedham was far enough out of Boston so that people mostly traveled through (paying tolls at the Dedham toll gates), leaving the citizenry relatively undisturbed. The one drawback to being accessible, but not too accessible, is that you may well get to have a jail in your town. Dedham houses the hoary Norfolk County Jail which, like its similarly appointed cousin in Concord, is set off by a large, forbidding wall.

25 Directions

START	Intersection of WASHINGTON ST. and HIGH ST., Dedham.
mi. 0.0	SOUTH on WASHINGTON ST.
0.3	RIGHT onto SCHOOL ST.
0.5	STRAIGHT onto AMES ST.
1.1	STRAIGHT onto PINE ST.
1.9	STRAIGHT onto NEEDHAM ST. (becomes GREAT PLAIN AVE., Needham)
3.1	RIGHT onto GREENDALE AVE.
5.0	RIGHT onto KENDRICK ST. (becomes NAHANTON ST., Newton)
6.8	RIGHT onto DEDHAM ST. (becomes BAKER ST., West Roxbury)
7.7	RIGHT into GETHSEMANE CEMETERY
7.8	REVERSE DIRECTION at CEMETERY OFFICE (= Brook Farm site)
7.9	RIGHT onto BAKER ST.
8.1	STRAIGHT on BAKER ST.
9.0	RIGHT onto SPRING ST. (becomes BRIDGE ST., Dedham)
9.5	STRAIGHT on BRIDGE ST. (at intersection with Ames St. and Pine St.)
10.9	LEFT onto COMMON ST.
11.0	BEAR LEFT onto HIGH ST. to
11.6	START.

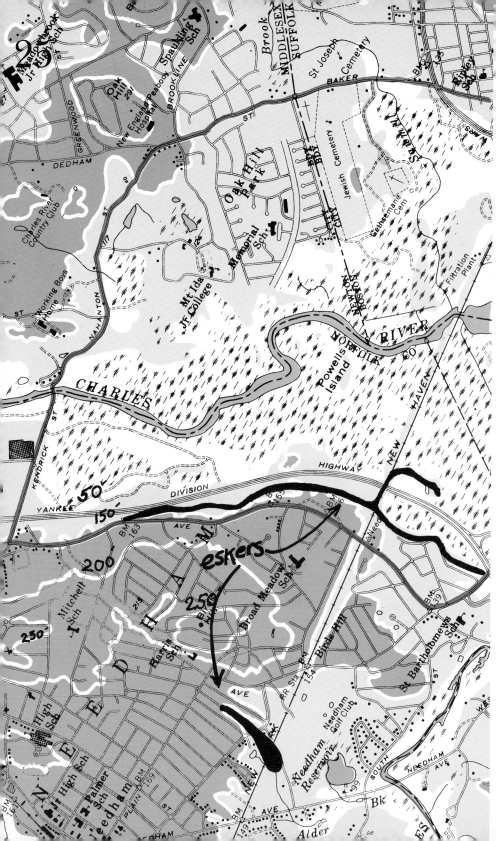

eskers

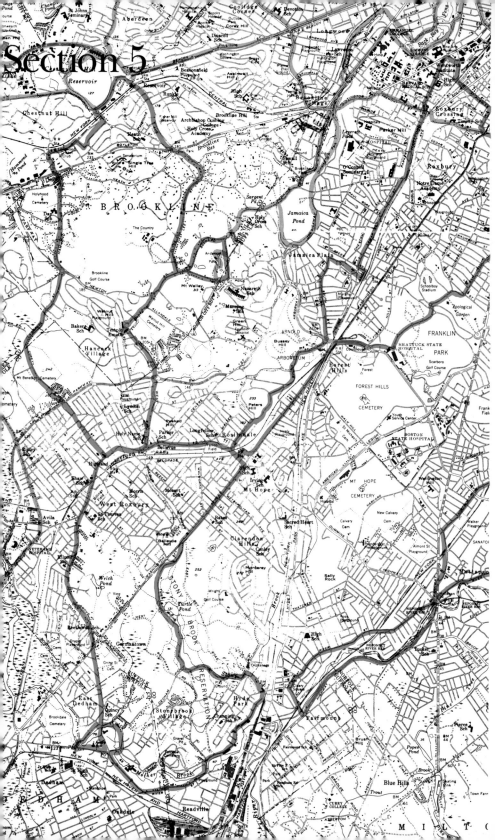

Section 5

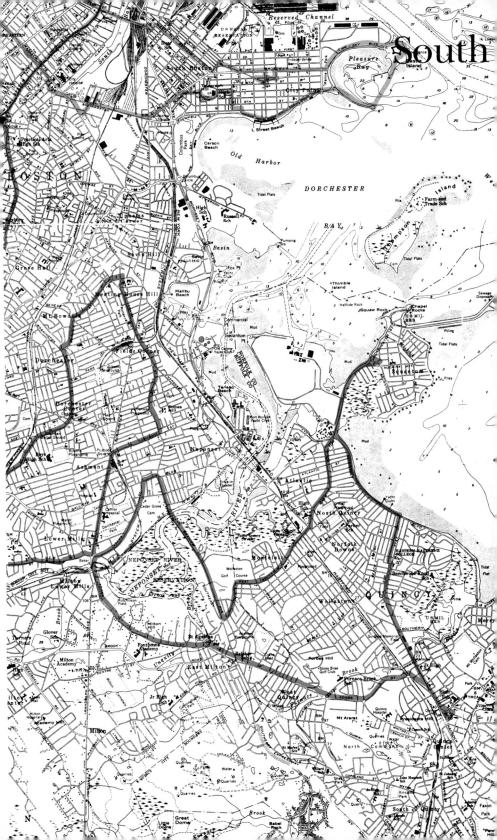

26 From Rocks to Riches

Brookline

Most of the bedrock in Brookline is Roxbury Conglomerate, the easiest to identify of all the rocks in the Boston area. This 'puddingstone,' as it is sometimes called, is made up of assorted pebbles, rocks, and boulders in a matrix of fine-grained sand which was solidified by heat and pressure deep underground. Close inspection suggests a product more like concrete than pudding, but the analogy is understandable. The ingredients were probably supplied by a glacier, from whose melting edge torrents of water carried a load of debris that had been caught up in the ice. The edge of the ice must have hovered over the Basin for some time, since a layer of sand and gravel several thousand feet thick was laid down here. When glacial melt-water was less turbulent, finer silt and clay particles settled out, later to become Cambridge Slate. Much of the slate has been eroded away but, being more resistant, a lot of the puddingstone held its position against the processes of weathering, providing the hills and outcroppings of Brookline.

As is the case with the highlands generally, these hills were developed late in the growth cycle of the city. The view is fine, but the climb consumes energy. Furthermore, the shallow soil cover means water supply problems and bedrock interference for many otherwise desirable building sites. When Boston first expanded onto the mainland following the first flush of European immigration, Brookline, at the eastern end of the Needham Uplands, remained the tip of a green peninsula jutting into an expanding suburban sea. So when post–Civil War development intensified the demand for building space, Brookline's wooded acres were still open for the wealthy in the market for country estates. Most of the mansions here represent one or another of the various late nineteenth- and early-twentieth century eclectic revival styles: Greek, Gothic, Queen Anne, Colonial, Georgian, Italian, and Medieval. The carriage house of the Larz Anderson estate, now the home of the Museum of Transportation, is a particularly elegant example. It is unusual in its faithfulness to the model, the Chaumont Castle in France.

The growth that effected Brookline was part of the vast westward expansion made necessary by the ever-increasing bulk and complexity of the capitalist system. The exploitation on a mammoth scale of the continent's natural resources was begun. Eager venture capital from East Coast cities such as Boston financed both the rail lines used to transport goods over the land, and the geologists needed to find the hidden treasures under it. This financial backing continued into the present century and is responsible for much of the basic geological knowledge of this country now available, and for the development of the theoretical framework on which it hangs. Supported by clients ranging from local building contractors to U.S. and foreign governments and corporations, the work of the famous geologists W. O. Crosby and his son I. B. Crosby is a case in point.

William Otis Crosby made his career in the development of techniques first for mineral extraction and later in the construction of dams, tunnels, aqueducts, and building projects (such as the foundation work for expanding MIT onto made-land sites). He also carved a place for himself in the annals of local geology with the publication in 1880 of *Contribution to the Geology of Eastern Massachusetts,* which was the only detailed and comprehensive treatment of the geology of this area for the next half century. He also began the systematic mapping of the Boston Basin on a large scale. Irving Ballard Crosby joined his father in a Cambridge-based consulting business in 1920 and then opened his own consulting firm on Beacon St. a few years later, specializing in dams and waterworks. He wrote 'The Earthquake Risk in Boston' and a series of articles for the *Boston Globe.*

Thus, it is partly because of the geological characteristics of the region that wealthy people settled in Brookline in the late 1800's, and it is partly because these, and other wealthy people, supported geological research that we understand how it came to be that way.

26 Directions

START   CLEVELAND CIRCLE, Brighton.

mi. 0.0   SOUTHEAST on CHESTNUT HILL AVE.

0.8   CROSS ROUTE 9 and BEAR LEFT onto LEE ST.

1.9   STRAIGHT onto CLYDE ST.

2.2   LEFT onto NEWTON ST.

2.3   LEFT onto GODDARD AVE.

2.9   RIGHT onto AVON ST.

3.3   RIGHT onto POND ST. (becomes NEWTON ST., Brookline)

4.1   BEAR LEFT onto GROVE ST.

4.6   RIGHT around ROTARY to third RIGHT onto WEST ROXBURY PARKWAY

5.9   RIGHT onto CENTRE ST.

6.0   RIGHT onto COREY ST.

7.1   RIGHT onto LAGRANGE ST.

8.5   RIGHT around ROTARY to second RIGHT onto HAMMOND ST.

8.9   RIGHT onto MIDDLESEX ST.

9.1   RIGHT onto CIRCUIT RD.

9.3   STRAIGHT onto SPOONER RD.

9.6   LEFT onto RESERVOIR RD.

9.7   RIGHT onto BEACON ST. to

10.3   START.

*Late 19th-century bicycles from the Museum of
Transportation, Brookline*

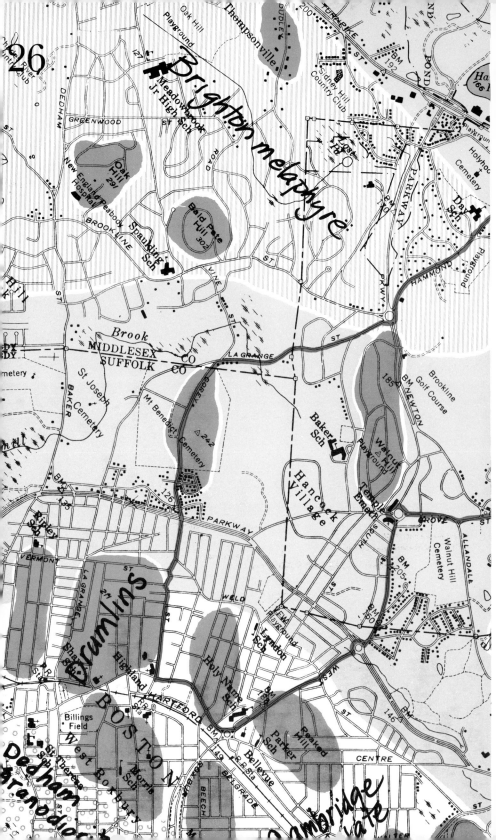

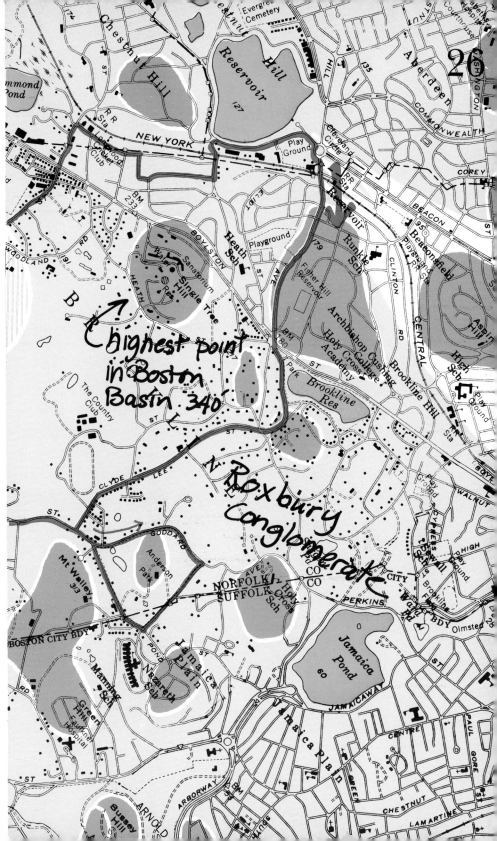

27 Out Behind the Water Shed

West Roxbury–Stony Brook

Stony Brook has its headwaters in the Stony Brook Reservation and from there flows north to the Charles River. Serious flooding in 1886 prompted a commission report on flood prevention tactics which, like all good commission reports, suggested both short-run and long-run possibilities. For the short run, culverts were constructed all over town to carry off the rainwater which had already swamped several hundred basements in Roxbury. For the long run, it was recognized that paved land simply didn't hold water very well and that large green areas were the best hedge against a rainy day. Hence the Stony Brook Reservation exists in part as a recreational area (Turtle Pond Parkway was finished in 1899), and in part as a watershed whose preservation was and is essential to prevent flooding further in town.

The Stony Brook Reservation occupies roughly the southeast quadrant of Bellevue Hill. The area is administered by the Metropolitan District Commission, itself formed in 1919 by the amalgamation of the Metropolitan Sewage, Water, and Parks Commissions. (The common interests of these three bodies, often involving the same pieces of land, made their merger inevitable.) The MDC has authority over all the land in Olmsted's Emerald Necklace (another large green flood control measure), including the parkways, as well as other lands relating to sewage and freshwater supplies in the Boston Basin. These include Quabbin Reservoir in the middle of the state, the sewage plants at Deer Island and off Squantum, the Middlesex Fells Reservation, and others.

The Mother Brook at Hyde Park is much like the Charles at

Newton Upper Falls in its mildly industrial flavor. (Plans to connect the Stony Brook and Neponset Reservations were left in abeyance at the turn of the century and there they remain to this day.) The industrial row along the river's edge is here seen in a moment of candor for what it is, and so labeled: Business Street. River Street follows Mother Brook to East Dedham. Here, close by the Charles, it was decreed in 1639 that 'a ditch should be dug at common charge through upper Charles River meadow unto East Brook [i.e., Mother Brook], that it may both be a partition fence in the same, and also may form a suitable creek unto a watermill, that it shall be found fitting to set a mill upon, in the opinion of a workman to be employed for that purpose.' Roughly a third of the Charles River is diverted into the Neponset via Mother Brook.

Centre St., West Roxbury, where this ride begins, is an interesting contrast to Washington St. Like most straight roads on the map, Washington St. dates from the turnpike era; like most really winding roads on the map, Centre St. harks back to earlier days when roads routinely went around hills and rarely over them. Centre St. threads a sinuous path through a cluster of drumlins. Since drumlins are always an excellent source of gravel, it will come as no surprise that this route takes you past the West Roxbury Sand and Gravel Company.

West Roxbury is just far enough out of town (though legally still part of the City of Boston) that a commuter train stops here. Compare this with Quincy and Newton, where defunct commuter lines were acquired by the Metropolitan Transit Authority (now the MBTA) and grafted onto existing lines in-town. The hills of Brookline to the north have sheltered West Roxbury to a certain extent from the expansion of the city, much as Bellevue Hill has sheltered Dedham.

27 Directions

START	Intersection of WEST ROXBURY PARKWAY and CENTRE ST., West Roxbury.
mi. 0.0	EAST on CENTRE ST.
0.2	BEAR RIGHT onto SOUTH ST.
0.7	RIGHT onto ROBERT ST.
0.9	BEAR LEFT onto CORINTH ST.
1.1	RIGHT onto WASHINGTON ST.
2.0	LEFT onto TURTLE POND PARKWAY
3.4	LEFT onto BALD KNOB RD.
4.0	RIGHT onto GORDON AVE.
4.3	STRAIGHT onto BUSINESS ST.
4.7	LEFT onto RIVER ST.
5.3	BEAR LEFT, then RIGHT (across brook) on RIVER ST.
5.9	RIGHT onto MILTON ST.
6.4	RIGHT onto MILL LANE
6.5	LEFT onto EMMETT AVE.
6.8	LEFT onto COLBURN ST.
6.9	STRAIGHT, then BEAR LEFT (across Bussey St.) on COLBURN ST.
7.3	LEFT onto HIGH ST.
7.6	LEFT onto BUSSEY ST. (becomes GROVE ST., West Roxbury)
9.1	BEAR RIGHT onto CENTRE ST. to
10.8	START.

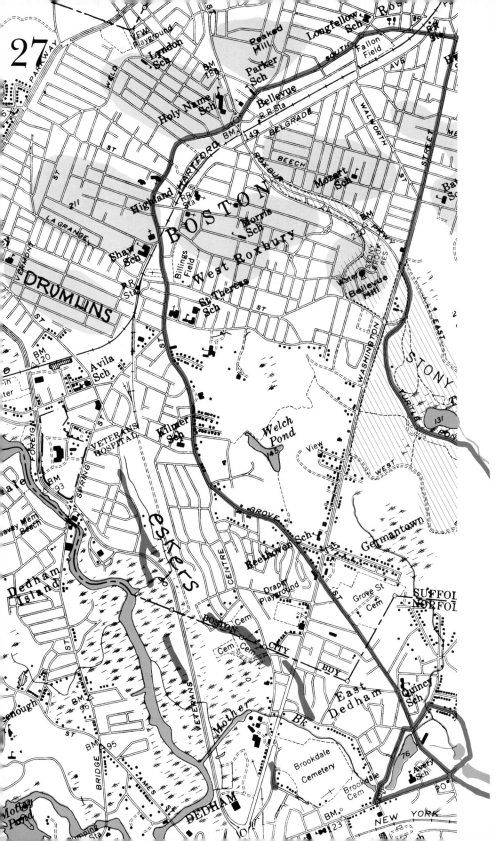

PARKWAY

VFW
Playground

Lyndon
Sch

Peaked
Hill

Longfellow Sch

SOUTH

Fallon
Field

Parker
Sch

Holy Name Sch

Bellevue
RR Sta

WALWORTH

AVE

BM 149

BELGRADE

BEECH

Mozart
Sch

ST

STREET

BM
189

WELD

LA GRANGE

ST

VERMONT

211

B·O·S·T·O·N

HIGHLAND

HARTFORD

RR
Sta

Morris
Sch

Belgrade

West Roxbury

210

PKWY

STONY BROOK RES

Water

Bellevue
Hill

Shaw
Sch

DRUMLINS

ST

RR
Sta

Billings
Field

St Theresa
Sch

ST

WASHINGTON

STONY

BM
120

Avila
Sch

Kilmer
Sch

EAST

ST

FOREIGN

ST

SPRING

VETERANS
HOSPITAL

Welch
Pond
145

View

WEST

131

BM
93

Davey Mem
Beach

GROVE

Beethoven Sch

Germantown

eskers

CENTRE

Draper
Playground

Grove St
Cem

SUFFOLK
NORFOLK

Dedham
Island

BOSTON Cem

CITY

Cem Cem

BDY

East
Dedham

Quincy
Sch

VETERANS

Mother

Bk

76

BM
96

BRIDGE

JAMES

ST

BM
95

Brookdale
Cemetery

Brookdale
Cem

Avery
Sch

PO

Moffatt
Pond

DEDHAM

BM
23

NEW YORK

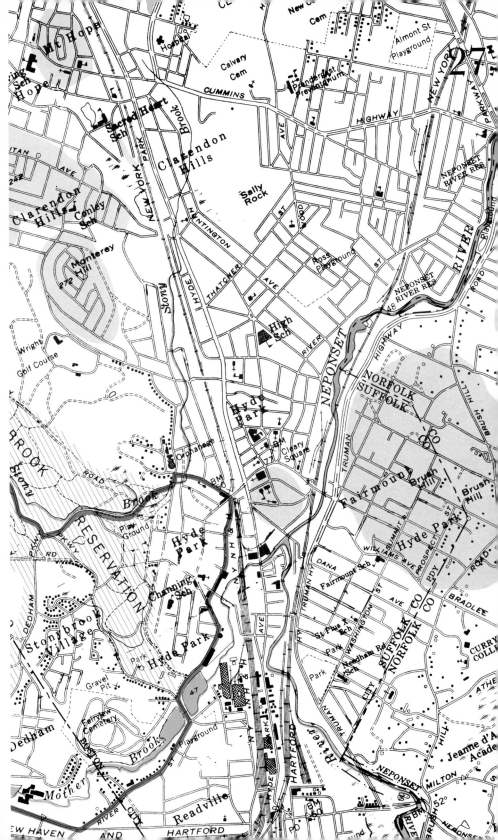

28 Fences

Roxbury–Jamaica Plain

Good fences, we are often told, make good neighbors. We are usually told this by someone who is content with both the location of the fence and the prospect of never getting to know the neighbors. This person is frequently disliked by his neighbors for his standoffishness and may be hated by them if the location or form of his fence is not to their liking.

Some fences can't be helped, of course: water is a natural fence between shores, and land occasionally separates the waterways at inconvenient places. Both of these age-old fences have been surmounted, where it seemed a good idea to do so, by building roads and canals to connect the waterways, and bridges to connect the shores where a ferry wouldn't do.

Unfortunately, roads, canals, and bridges can themselves act as fences where formerly none existed. A low bridge had better be a drawbridge if the water which it spans is to be used for travel, and a canal which can't be crossed might as well be an ocean. Ironically, it has been in his attempts to cross the greatest natural fence, sheer long distance, that man has created his worst local fences. The railroads, and their offspring, the high-speed roads, have made it possible to travel practically anywhere in record time but to the other side of the thoroughfare, a canal with no crossing.

The area covered in this ride is divided down the middle by a railroad. To the east lies a series of additional fences: heavily trafficked streets, the dark and deafening elevated railway, more railroads, and a fair number of steep hills. This is Roxbury, the heart of Boston's Black community.

To the west of the central track lies Jamaica Plain. This community too is fragmented by a series of natural and manmade fences: hills, horrendous intersections, and major thoroughfares. To the south, Roxbury and Jamaica Plain are bounded by hills, parks, and cemeteries (the latter, fenced), and to the north, by a hopeless tangle of virtually impassible roads, trolley lines, and railroads. This section of Jamaica Plain is largely inhabited by poor whites. A substantial community of Spanish-speaking people is found in both Jamaica Plain and Roxbury, separated to a great extent from their neighbors by yet another kind of fence, a linguistic one.

While it is often more difficult to leap these manmade fences than it is the natural obstacles to which they ordinarily owe their existence, it is seldom impossible, and it is frequently worth the effort involved. For one thing, you get to see for yourself what it looks like on (and from) both sides of the fence instead of having to rely on what others (who may never have visited there themselves) have had to say about the 'other' side. For some, this whole ride will be on the 'other' side of the fence; for others, only the part where the people of the other color or language live will seem at all exotic. And for those very few to whom nothing human is alien, there is the Franklin Park Zoo and the Arnold Arboretum.

28 Directions

8.7	RIGHT onto LAMARTINE ST. (no sign)
9.7	LEFT onto HEATH ST.
9.8	RIGHT onto BROMLEY ST., then
9.9	RIGHT, then LEFT onto TERRACE ST.
10.3	CROSS TREMONT ST. onto GURNEY ST.
10.4	RIGHT onto PARKER ST. to
10.8	START.

Fort Hill, Roxbury

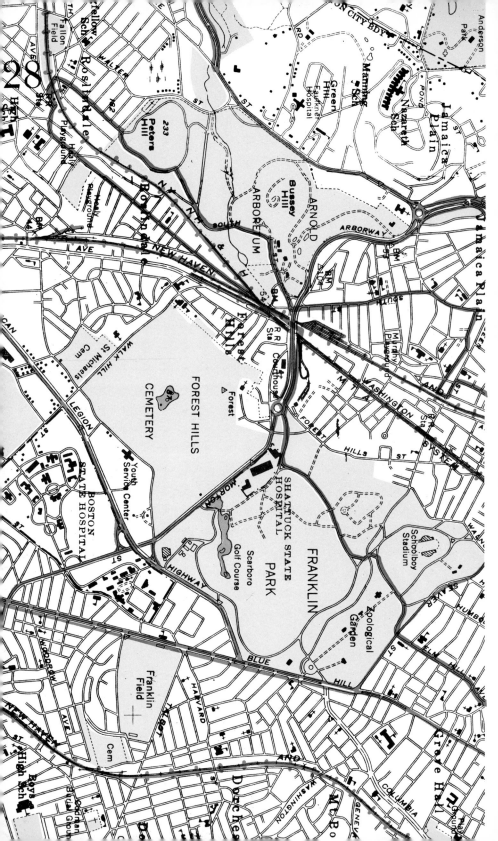

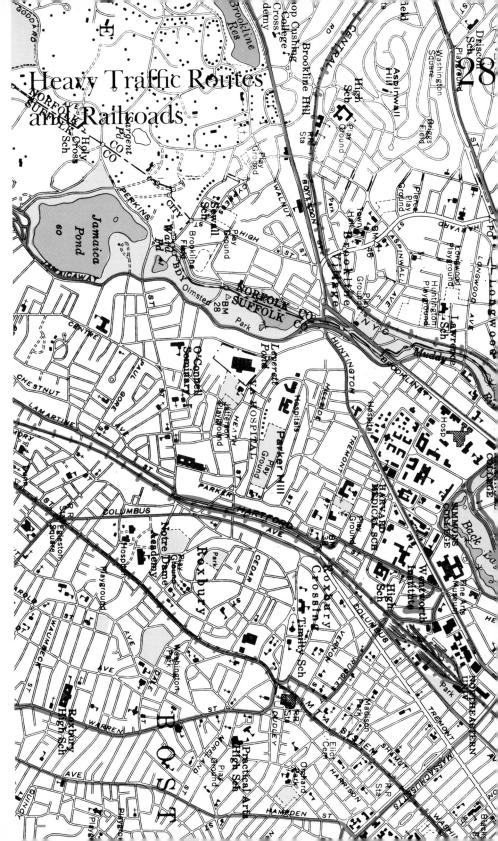

Heavy Traffic Routes
and Railroads

28

29 Triple-Decker Delight

Dorchester–Hyde Park

Imagine 1910. Republican William H. Taft, former President Teddy Roosevelt's Secretary of War, succeeded him to the presidency a year ago. Business has been more or less OK for about twenty years now, a relief from the depression of 1873–1885 that marked the collapse of the post–Civil War economy. If you happen to be a member of Boston's rapidly expanding labor force, you have a slightly better than average chance of being white-collar. True, white-collar jobs are multiplying at the lower ranks (sales/clerical) rather than higher up the socio-economic ladder (professional/managerial), but still, with a little care, you might save a thousand or two. With that kind of money, you're not about to enter the arena of international big business, but you could easily get a mortgage and build a triple-decker in Dorchester.

When you ride this route, think 3-D. Look down the many long, straight side streets and enjoy the texture which emerges from the evenly spaced, evenly set back, evenly tall buildings. You may not find the architectural refinement of the Back Bay, but then neither will you find its pretentiousness. You'll see whole areas where the buildings clearly display their age, and you may lament the urban decay which seems to accompany high-density housing. But before you blame population density alone, remember the vast stretches of this route where the triple-deckers are in perfect repair, though equally densely populated.

Differences in the state of repair/disrepair provide only one of the many elements which modulate the visual impact of triple-deckerland. There are streets with every house the same, followed by more streets exactly the same. There are streets with minor variations on the theme grouped in segments of two or three houses. Whole areas of this sort are then bounded by streets with a mixture of housing types. The single-family houses on corner lots were built by optimistic Yankees in the first suburban rush to escape the new Irish immigrants in central Boston.

A generation later, the immigrant baby boom swept through Dorchester. The expanding population raised both land prices and building heights, causing former residents to leapfrog over Dorchester in their search for neighbors of their own social status. Toward the Neponset River, you'll see a more recent version of a strip of mixed housing types, evidence of the continuing expansion of Boston and of its status hierarchy. The sharp-eyed will notice the almost obliterated evidence of a much earlier instance of the same phenomenon in the relationship of colonial Meetinghouse Hill to later Codman Square.

The almost complete lack of any commercial or industrial activity in the center of triple-deckerland reveals its turn-of-the-century bedroom community origins. After 1900, the street cars in this area were electrified and the triple-decker really came into its own, though there are a few scattered 3-D prototypes closer to town dating back to the acceleration of building in the 1880's. As early as 1850, land speculators put in horsecars on the old stagecoach route down Dorchester Ave. to Lower Mills, but electric trolleys were fast enough for the fleeing Yankees to be able to move the next step out from Boston and, indeed, helped to chase them from the noisy corner lots.

With rapid mass transit extended to the first open zone beyond Boston's fire laws, which prohibited three-family wooden structures, the area was rapidly and almost uniformly developed. Then, as now, roughly 25 percent of the buildings were owner-occupied, with occasional pockets of more than twice that. Almost all residents still live in one kind of family group or another. Three families stacked up may be dense, but it's not necessarily crowded, especially when you consider the social isolation of those who stay home in single-family commuterville.

29 Directions

START	MATTAPAN SQUARE, Mattapan.
mi. 0.0	NORTH on BLUE HILL AVE.
0.1	BEAR RIGHT onto BABSON ST.
0.6	BEAR RIGHT onto NORFOLK ST. (at Anslow Sq.)
2.1	BEAR RIGHT onto TALBOT ST., then LEFT onto WASHINGTON ST. (at Codman Sq.)
2.7	RIGHT onto BOWDOIN ST.
3.5	BEAR RIGHT onto CHURCH ST. (at Coppins Sq.), then LEFT, then RIGHT across ADAMS ST. on CHURCH ST.
3.6	RIGHT onto WINTER ST. (Meetinghouse Hill), then
3.7	LEFT onto ADAMS ST.
4.5	BEAR RIGHT on ADAMS ST. (Neponset Ave. forks left)
5.1	RIGHT onto ASHMONT ST.
5.6	LEFT onto DORCHESTER AVE. (MBTA Ashmont Station)
6.6	RIGHT onto WASHINGTON ST., then next
6.7	LEFT onto RIVER ST.
8.0	CROSS BLUE HILL AVE. on RIVER ST.
9.6	LEFT onto FAIRMOUNT AVE.
9.9	LEFT onto TRUMAN HIGHWAY
11.4	STRAIGHT around ROTARY onto BLUE HILL AVE. to
11.6	START.

A triple-decker in Dorchester

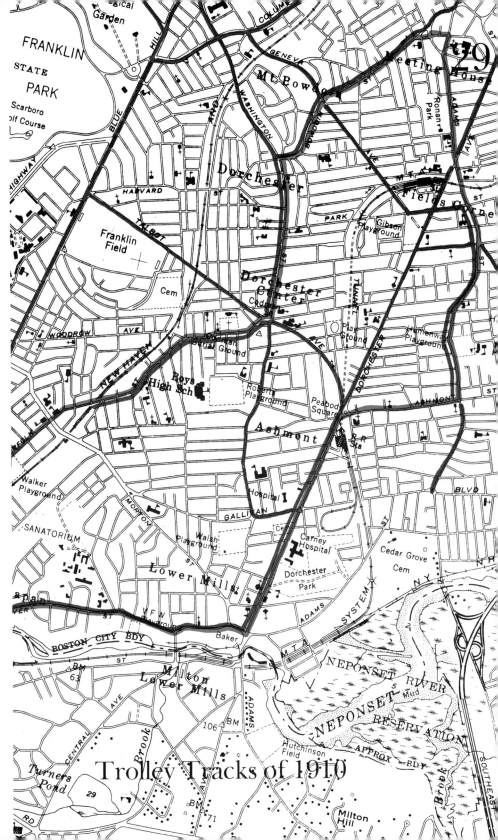

Trolley Tracks of 1910

30 Taken for Granite

Quincy–Milton Lower Mills

The rock display on the front of the New England Cut Stone Co. building encourages riders-by to think about applied bedrock geology as they cross the Neponset River on Granite St. into Quincy. On the other hand, the scenery for the next few miles brings the mind up from such geological depths. Starting with the Neponset estuary itself, most of the surrounding landscape tells more about the glacier which once covered this area than about the bedrock which underlies it. The broad estuary with its typical salt marsh vegetation is, for example, a river valley which has lost some ground relative to sea level. Exhibit A in the case of New England's 'drowned coast,' it is one of the bits of evidence linking the ups and downs of the coastline to the comings and goings of the last glacier.

Sea level dropped as glacial advance froze an increasing share of the earth's water supply into the continental ice sheet. At the same time, land level dropped as the earth's crust sank under the immense weight of the glacier. When the glacier melted, the sea rose faster than the land sprang back. Before the slow-moving crust finished its upswing out of the ocean, the marine clay now found above sea level in parts of the Boston Basin was deposited. The crust is now in a local downswing in its recovery from glacial retreat, as is shown by the 'drowning' of the mouth of the Neponset by salt water. A little later on, the route offers some spectacular views of Exhibit B, the islands of Boston Harbor. These islands are drumlins, formed when both land and sea were near their lowest levels, and then submerged by the rising ocean. Caught between complete submergence and higher ground, these drumlins have been robbed of much of their seaward slopes by beach-building waves.

Glaciers don't move backwards; they retreat by melting faster than they move forward. Nobody knows why forward movement grinds to a halt and melting speeds up when it does, but the effects of these changes are readily observable. In fact, you can't help observing them as you pedal over a few eskers on West Squantum Street. The shape of these eskers reflects the shape of the vast drainage system which returned glacial melt-water to the sea. The northerly retreat of the glacier left behind these long, narrow, parallel piles of debris from the channels in the melting ice.

The native granite of the 'Church of the Presidents' in Quincy is a reminder of the solid bedrock foundation which underlay relatively recent glacial events. After circling the church and heading for Milton on Adams St., however, you'll pass over three different kinds of bedrock whose relationship to each other has been readjusted by the Appalachian Revolution. Besides familiar Roxbury pudding-stone, the route crosses a small patch of Braintree slate and a corner of the famous Quincy granite which stretches off the map to the Blue Hills. (This formation was excluded from the Basin in early geologic maps of the area but is now considered to be *inside* the Basin, and the title of 'Southern Boundary Fault' has been moved to a fault south of the Blue Hills.) This granite, or, depending on how you look at it, the Battle of Bunker Hill, was the immediate reason for building the first American railroad. A tramway depending on horse and ox power, it was used to transport quarried granite to the Neponset on its way to the Bunker Hill Monument in 1826.

When you finish looking back over the beginning of the route while resting from the climb up Milton Hill, you may wish to visit the Museum of the American China Trade before coasting down to Milton Lower Mills. If you go, you'll see some of the luxurious artifacts which wealthy Bostonians spent their money on in the early 1800's, and at the same time follow up the humble start of American railroading. The museum is in the old house of R. B. Forbes, who was one of a small group of kinsmen led by his brother, J. M. Forbes, into redirecting capital accumulated in the China trade before the Opium War (1839–1842) into fruitful railroad investment. Until the Forbes group became active in the mid-1840's, investment in railroads in

Massachusetts was largely confined to local lines such as the Boston & Lowell Railroad which served the needs of industrialists who had gotten out of foreign trade a generation earlier.

The Forbes group started out investing speculatively in railroads promoted by others, but were soon protecting their growing capital by direct management of the long-term growth of their own railroad system. Like the textile manufacturers before them, the Forbes group developed a commitment to an expanding population — in this case, to fill the West as fast as railroads could be built. The rivalry between North and South over who was going to develop the West (and in whose image) was reflected in the active part played by the Forbes group behind the scenes in abolition politics and in running the Civil War.

Church of the Presidents, Quincy

30 Directions

START   Intersection of ADAMS ST. and DORCHES-
TER AVE., Milton Lower Mills.

mi. 0.0   NORTHEAST on ADAMS ST.

0.9   RIGHT onto GALLIVAN BLVD. then

1.0   RIGHT onto GRANITE ST.

2.5   LEFT onto W. SQUANTUM ST. (first traffic lights)

3.9   CROSS HANCOCK ST. onto E. SQUANTUM ST.

4.9   CROSS QUINCY SHORE DRIVE on E. SQUANTUM ST.

5.5   CIRCLE ROTARY at HUCKINS AVE. and return to QUINCY SHORE DR.

6.3   LEFT onto QUINCY SHORE DR.

7.3   RIGHT onto W. ELM ST. (first lights after yacht clubs)

7.8   STRAIGHT onto ELM ST.

8.1   LEFT onto HANCOCK ST.

9.3   LEFT onto TEMPLE ST. (First Parish Church) then immediately
LEFT onto WASHINGTON ST. (circling church) then immediately

9.4   RIGHT onto HANCOCK ST.

9.6   LEFT onto ADAMS ST.

11.6   RIGHT onto GRANITE ST. then immediately
LEFT over bridge then immediately

11.8   RIGHT onto ADAMS ST.

12.3   BEAR RIGHT on ADAMS ST. (at sign for the Museum of the American China Trade) to

13.4   START.

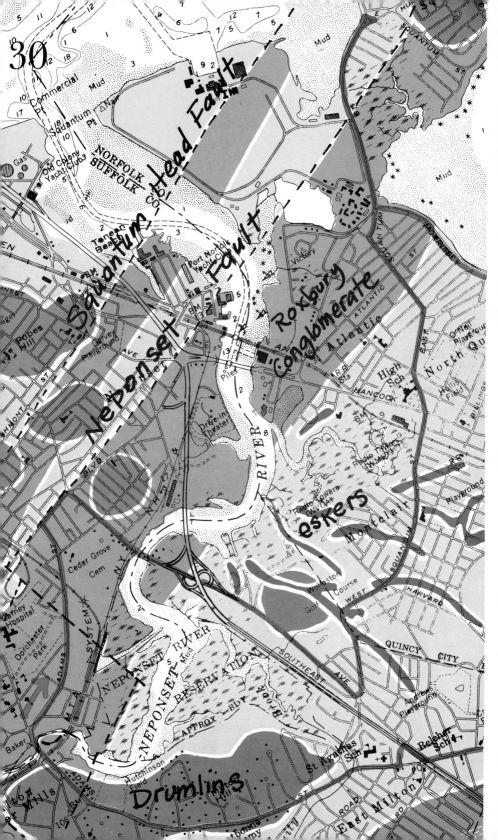

QUINCY

BAY

Tidal Flat

Tidal Flat

Yacht Clubs

BLVD

Adam Shor

EASTERN NAZARENE COLLEGE

MORRISSEY BLVD

PARK

Black Cr

15 SHORE

AVE

Merrymount

Parker Sch

Beechwood Knoll Sch

MERRYMOUNT

Pine

Blacks Cr

SEAL

Mt Wollaston Cem

US NAV RESERV

Broa

Norfolk Downs

Cambridge Slate

ST

US MIL RES

BM 32

ELM

BEACH

BM 15

HARTFORD

Wollaston

SOUTHERN

ARTERY

BM 10

SOUTHERN

BM 8

YMCA

NEWPORT

ST

Soldiers Memorial Field

AVE

BM 19

BM 23

Armory

Jr High Sch

High Sch

BM

BEALE

ST

Brook

Furnace Brook

17

ST

PKWY

BM

40

HANCOCK

Forbes Hill

Stony Brae Golf Club

BROOK

Furnace Brook Sch

Quincy Hospital

Quincy Center

Presidents Hill

Cranch Sch

Quincy Center

Cem

Ch

West Quincy

ADAMS

Braintree slate (interbedded with surrounding rock)

Mt Ararat

WHITWELL

CRANCH ST

Water

GRANITE

Bk

St Jos

FURNACE

WILLARD

Quarries

QUARRY

Quincy granite

or

ST

John Hancock Sch

WATER

Kincaid Park

STREET

FURNACE

COMMON

ST JOS

Index